Octopus and Squid

JAMES C. HUNT

MONTEREY BAY AQUARIUM

Monterey, California

The purpose of the Monterey Bay Aquarium is to stimulate interest, increase knowledge and promote stewardship of Monterey Bay and the world's ocean environment through innovative exhibits, public education and scientific research. One goal lies behind all we do: to help protect the world's oceans.

Acknowledgments I wish to thank Steven Webster, Judith Connor, Jessica Bridges, Nora Deans, and Lisa Tooker for their efforts in reviewing and producing this book. I also thank Bruce Robison, William Hamner, Kim Reisenbichler, and the captain and crew of the R/V *Point Lobos* for their support and encouragement while at the Monterey Bay Aquarium Research Institute.

Published in the United States by the Monterey Bay Aquarium Foundation, 886 Cannery Row, Monterey, CA 93940-1085 http://www.mbayaq.org.
Library of Congress Cataloging in Publication Data: TK

Photos and Illustration Credits:

Cover: Steve Rosenberg

Back Cover: Doug Perrine/Innerspace Visions (top), Fred Bavendam (bottom)

Bank, Marjorie/Mo Yung Productions: 39 (top left)

Bavendam, Fred: 4, 6 (top), 9 (top right), 13, 15 (top), 16 (top), 18 (bottom), 20 (top right), 28 (bottom), 29 (top), 30 (bottom), 31 (bottom), 32 (top), 39 (top right)

Caudle, Ann: 15 (middle), 28 (top), 30 (top), 46 (bottom), 48 (middle)

Chamberlain, Marc C.: 7 (top right), 23, 43 (middle)

Conlin, Mark: 18 (top right), 27 (middle)

Courtesy of Monterey Bay Aquarium Research Institute: 21 (middle)

Courtesy of National Geographic Society Image Collection: 47 (inset photo)

Courtesy of The Mariners Museum, Newport News, Virginia: 60, 61 (top left)

Davis, Chuck: 26 (top)

Foott, Jeff: 17 (bottom), 27 (bottom), 42, 43 (top)

Forsythe, John: 29 (bottom)

Hall, Howard/HHP: 1, 5 (top & bottom), 12 (bottom right), 14 (bottom), 17 (middle), 45 (top left), 49 (bottom)

Hall, Michele/HHP: 7 (top left), 8 (bottom), 11 (top), 14 (top left)

Leggitt, Marjorie C.: 53, 54

Lisin, Susan: 33 (bottom right)

Martinez, Andrew J.: 19 (top)

Monterey Bay Aquarium: 7 (bottom), 11 (top), 20 (top left), 21 (top), 24-25 (bottom), 34-35, 46 (top), 48 (top), 61 (right)

Perrine, Doug/Innerspace Visions: 8 (top), 12 (bottom left), 36 (top), 38, 41 (bottom)

Reisenbichler, Kim: 22, 33 (bottom left), 55, 59, 62

Robison, Bruce: 50 (top)

Roessler, Carl: 5 (middle), 19 (bottom)

Rosenberg, Steve: 11 (bottom), 18 (top left)

Seaborn, Charles: 10 (bottom), 14 (top left)

Seki, Katsunore: 57 (bottom)

Snyderman, Marty: 9 (top left), 15 (bottom), 20 (bottom), 25 (top), 27 (top)

Westmorland, F. Stuart: 9 (bottom), 31 (top), 37, 45 (top right)

Wilder, Randy/Monterey Bay Aquarium: 47 (background photo)

Wrobel, David J.: 10 (top), 16 (bottom), 17 (top), 31 (top), 32 (bottom), 36 (bottom), 49 (top), 51, 52, 56 (top)

Wu, Norbert: 31 (middle), 40, 41 (top), 44

Managing Editor: Nora L. Deans
Project Editor: Lisa M. Tooker
Series Design: James Stockton & Associates
Art Director: Ann W. Douden
Book Design: Archetype, Inc.
Printed in Hong Kong by Global Interprint

Contents

In the dimly lit waters of a cold, rocky coast, a dark shape half-glides, half-crawls over the seafloor. Eight long sucker-lined arms lightly feel along the rocks and crevices, sensing and "tasting" everything it passes as it hunts for crabs and shrimps.

Alarmed by a sudden movement, vivid colors flash across the animal's body and it's gone, jetting away so quickly you wonder if you imagined it in the first place.

Octopus

This wily animal's life depends on its mastery of stealth and disguise. Like other octopuses, it can remain hidden from all but the most discerning eye while sitting out in plain view. Look again, carefully. That bumpy looking rock just moved.

Often curious and even playful, octopuses are at once intriguing and amusing to watch. Most children have heard about the intelligence of octopuses, but few adults realize that octopuses have a larger brain-size to body-weight ratio than any invertebrate animal.

At first glance, we can see why the octopus is known as a master of disguise, able to change color in an instant to match its surroundings. If that tactic fails to fool a predator, the octopus can disappear in a cloud of ink ejected from its body. Yet closer inspection reveals that octopuses also can change the texture of their skin and can shape their ink to echo their own body image and thus serve as a decoy.

Cuttlefish

In the following pages, you'll discover the amazing variety of octopuses, squids, and cuttlefishes that crawl, swim or glide like ghosts in almost every ocean habitat. You'll meet animals that glow in the dark, eject ink, are highly venomous, highly intelligent, live alone or in groups, were thought to have gone extinct with the dinosaurs, change color in the blink of an eye, use jets to move and even to "fly," are active predators and important prey, and all belong to the group of animals known as cephalopods.

Octopus

1

Head-footed Animals

Throughout history, octopuses and their cephalopod relatives have fueled our imaginations. Bizarre and elusive, their life histories loomed larger than life until scientists slowly unraveled the true stories. Only now, with technologies that let us study them in their own watery realm, are we beginning to understand this complex group of sea creatures.

The paper nautilus (top) has an external shell that is thin and delicate.

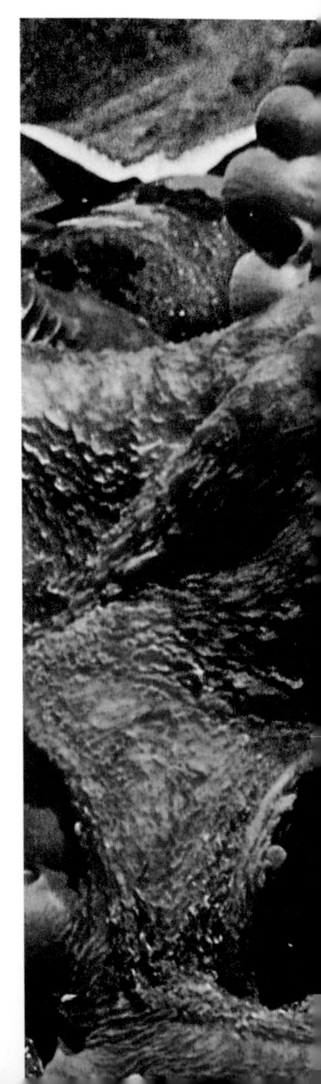

Living cephalopods include octopuses, squids, cuttlefishes, the chambered nautilus, and a unique species found only in the deep sea called the vampire squid *(Vampyroteuthis)*, even though it is not really a squid. *Vampyroteuthis* is a "living fossil," which means it can tell us a lot about other living cephalopods because it has some features similar to octopuses, some features similar to squids, and some unique features that may represent characteristics of extinct cephalopods, providing a living link to the past.

To fully understand cephalopods, you need to know they belong to a larger group of animals called molluscs, which includes snails, slugs, clams, scallops, oysters, and mussels. Molluscs have a hollow body space called a mantle cavity. Water passes through this space and over the gills for respiration. Molluscs also have a meaty foot, which has become very different among the cephalopod groups. In cephalopods, what was originally the foot has become the head, arms, and sometimes the tentacles. Cephalopod actually means "head foot."

Cephalopods are entirely marine—no cephalopod has ever lived in fresh water like some of their distant relatives—clams and snails. Some live near the surface of the sea or in the intertidal zone. During low tide, you may find octopuses hiding in tide pools awaiting the return of high tide. Cephalopods also live in cold, dark submarine canyons in the deepest parts of the ocean where they may never see any sunlight.

In every species of cephalopod, there are male and female sexes. Sometimes both sexes are similar in size and appearance, but in some species, like the unusual octopus called the argonaut or paper nautilus (*Argonauta*), the difference is great. The female may be over a foot in length and secretes a thin, paper-like calcareous shell while the male is only one-inch long and does not secrete a shell.

Cephalopods have a beak which is similar in shape to a parrot's beak. The mouth contains a hard-scraping tongue called a radula. When a cephalopod seizes another animal, the beak or radula penetrates hard shells or breaks bone. Often, poison is injected into the

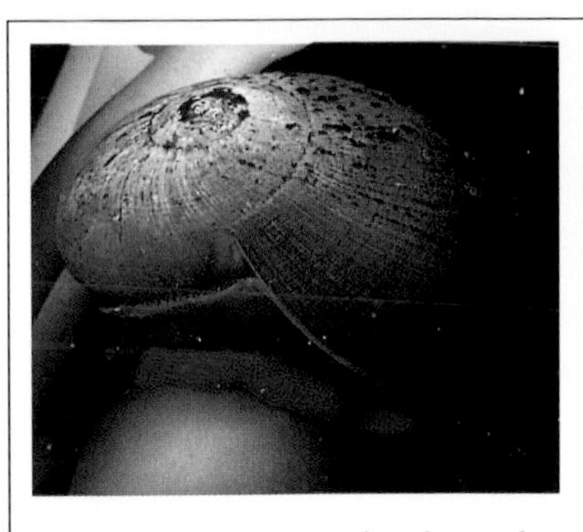

prey from salivary glands in the cephalopod. They are active and agile hunters, moving swiftly through the water or along the sea bottom in search of food. Cephalopods are important predators, eating fishes, shrimp, crabs, clams and other hard-shelled sea life, worms, and even other cephalopods.

A hallmark of cephalopods is jet propulsion. Cephalopods have a tube-shaped organ called a siphon or funnel. They also have a muscular body or mantle surrounding all the internal organs that are attached to the inside of the mantle. There is open space around

The top snail (top left) and conch (top right) have hard shells and skeletons.

This giant octopus glides along the seafloor in search of food (bottom).

the internal organs called the mantle cavity, and an opening on either side of the head to allow seawater into the mantle cavity. The siphon exhales water, which has been drawn through the mantle cavity and passed over the gills. The next time you see an octopus, watch how it breathes. You can see the openings on the sides of the head draw water into the body and then see the siphon push the water out again.

However, cephalopods also can close the openings into the mantle cavity and, by contracting all of the mantle muscles at the same time, push the water trapped inside the body out through the siphon with great force. This results in a quick burst of acceleration and speed. Jet propulsion may be a means of locomotion or an escape behavior. Octopuses and squids often eject a blob of ink through the siphon as they jet away, virtually disappearing in a puff of ink.

An octopus' sharp, hard beak (top left) can crush the strong shells of their prey. An octopus exhales through its siphon (top right). Octopuses come in an enormous range of sizes from octopuses an inch long (bottom) to twice the size of a human diver (right).

Endless Varieties There are over 600 species of cephalopods, and that number increases every year as marine biologists discover new species. Cephalopods come in a huge range of sizes, from tiny cuttlefishes and octopuses no bigger than your thumbnail to the North Pacific giant octopus *(Octopus dolfleini)*, reported at lengths up to 30 feet and weights of nearly 600 pounds. Bigger still is the giant squid *(Architeuthis dux)* which reaches 60 feet in length and weighs over half-a-ton. The eyes of giant squid are as large as volleyballs, the largest of any animal ever to live on our planet—larger than the eyes of dinosaurs or even the mighty blue whale!

Intelligence and Nerves Cephalopods have a large and complex nervous system. They have the most developed and complex brain of any invertebrate animals. The relative size of the cephalopod brain is often larger than that of fishes. Much of this great size in squids is attributable to two large optic lobes and testifies to the importance of vision in these active, open-ocean hunters. Octopuses

Octopuses use jet propulsion to gently glide through the water or escape in rapid bursts of acceleration (top left). Octopuses use ink as a visual and chemical defense against predators (top right).

have a brain designed to recognize and remember the feel or texture of things, which fits their life along the seafloor.

The intelligence of octopuses has been the source of study for many decades. Although it is difficult to compare or even define exactly what we mean by the "intelligence" of an animal, those biologists who have attempted such studies compare the intelligence of octopuses to that of fishes and even some birds.

The cephalopod brain also controls the huge array of nerve cells and intricate nervous systems associated with the complex color changes of the skin. Each of the hundreds of patterns and color combinations produced in cephalopods is the result of thousands of colored cells, each with associated muscles, all under nervous control.

The nervous system of squids has given us our understanding of how nerves work in all animals, including human beings. The reason for this comes from work inspired by the noted cephalopod neuro-physiologist Dr. J. Z. Young. He encouraged biologists who were trying to determine how nerves function to use a squid's giant nerve cells. Squids have a set of special nerve cells, which are larger than any in the animal kingdom. These nerves may be up to one

Octopuses can color and shape their skin to disappear into the background. They may also flash colors to startle a predator and allow a brief moment for escape (left).

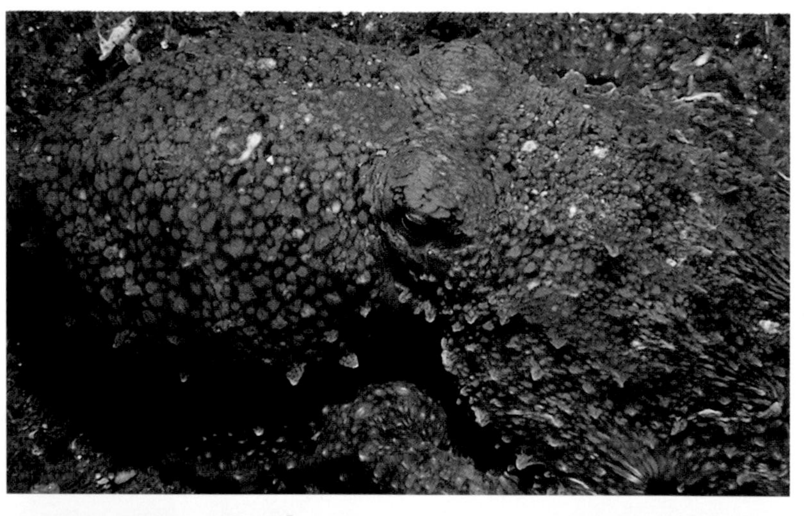

millimeter in diameter, making them as easily seen by the human eye as a piece of thin spaghetti. In comparison, our nerves and those of other vertebrates are very tiny. This has to do with the anatomy of the nerves themselves. In vertebrates, nerve cells have a special sheath called myelin, which helps to direct the electric impulses that allow nerves to work. Invertebrates lack myelin around their nerves and in order to quickly and efficiently conduct electric impulses, invertebrate nerves have to be large.

Why do squids need to efficiently conduct impulses? Squids need to control the thrust of water through their siphons for jet propulsion. A large push of water results in a quick burst of speed and allows the squid to escape danger. But this large push requires the mantle to contract all at once. In order to achieve this synchrony, giant nerve fibers run along both sides of the mantle, conducting their electric impulses with great speed and efficiency.

We owe a great debt to the squid for its giant nerves. Advances in the search for cures of nervous diseases like multiple sclerosis, which attack the myelin of nerves come directly and indirectly from research on the structure and function of a squid's giant nerve cell.

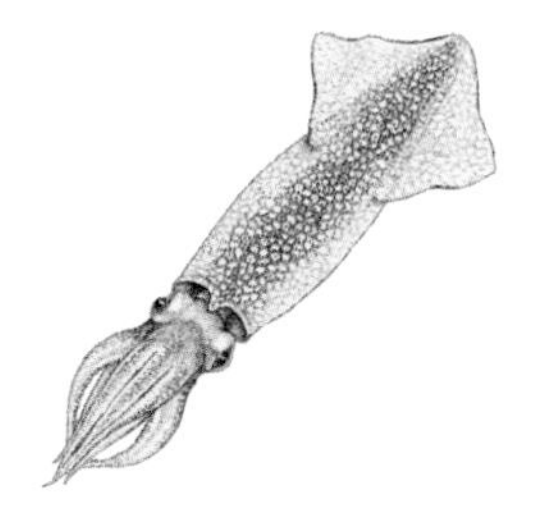

Market squid

The arms of squid curl back in preparation for attacking their prey (bottom).

2

Octopus and Kin

In virtually every animal group known, novel species and exceptions abound. This reflects the wonderful diversity of creatures inhabiting our world, and is one of the most exciting aspects of studying biology. Cephalopods are no exception. Each of the major groups differs greatly from the other, and reflects the way the group lives, hunts, mates and cares for young.

This octopus (right) has retreated into its den to feed. After eating, it discards the empty shells outside the entrance forming a pile or midden.

Octopuses Snorkeling over a coral reef, a diver spots a pile of broken shells in front of a small hollow. Closer inspection reveals that the shells are nearly perfect except for a single, tiny hole in each. The diver peers into the hollow and sees nothing at first, but then notices along the top of the hole a single row of tiny suckers. This is the den of an octopus. The diver gently reaches a gloved hand into the hole, but suddenly cannot see. Brown, opaque water swirls everywhere. After the water clears, the hole is empty and the octopus is nowhere to be seen. It is hiding nearby but by this time its skin so closely resembles the surrounding reef that the diver has little hope of seeing the octopus again.

From shallow tide pools to the world's deep oceans, octopuses have become one of the most successful and important groups of animals in the sea. Most people are familiar with the appearance of the typical reef octopus. Two eyes with w-shaped pupils sit atop the head, next to what many children call the "nose," but is actually the mantle. On either side of the mantle, behind the eyes, are the openings into

As the octopus crawls over the reef, it changes skin color to match the colors of corals (bottom left). Octopuses can also sculpt their skin into various textures resembling their surroundings (bottom right).

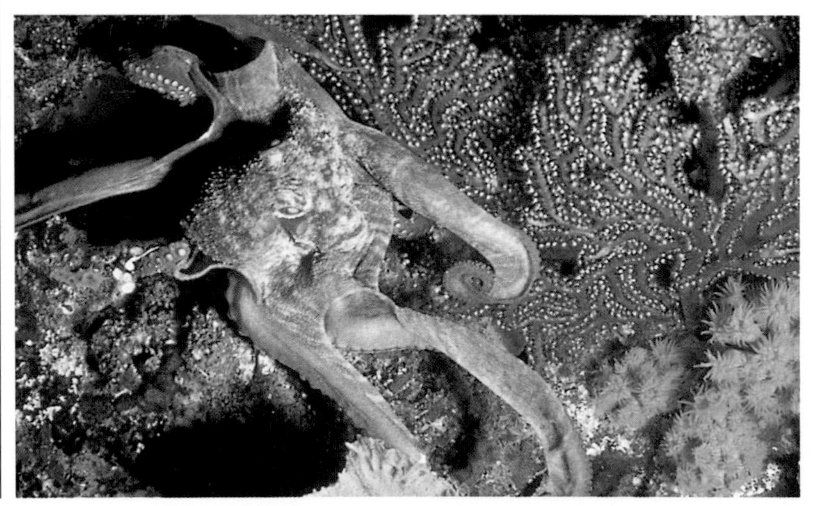

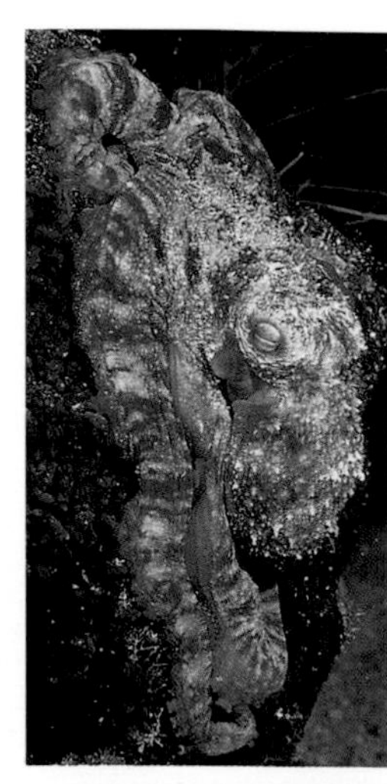

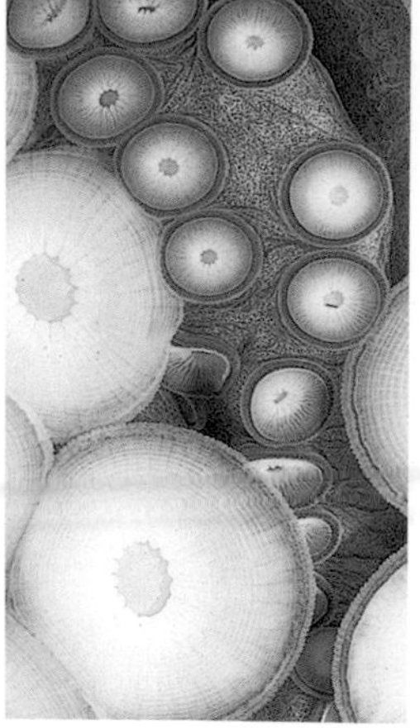

the mantle cavity. Water is drawn in through these openings, passed over the gills, and ejected through the siphon below the head. And, of course, those eight arms are a dead give-away.

The arms lined with one or two rows of suckers, extend away from the bottom of the head. The suckers are cup-shaped and the rim of each sucker is smooth and elastic. A complex series of muscles and nerves controls each sucker individually and together the suckers can provide a powerful grip, or can be used to crawl along almost any surface. Thousands of taste receptors and millions of texture receptors line each sucker rim. Octopuses are probably the most sophisticated animals in the world when it comes to the texture of objects. Yet studies report that they have difficulty determining the weight of objects. In an octopus' world of groping through cracks and crevices with sinuous arms, the feel of what each arm contacts is vital to the animal. Remembering taste and texture is the most important thing for the survival of an octopus.

Octopuses usually live along the bottom of the ocean. They inhabit rocky areas, coral reefs or sandy seafloors. Stories abound about the clever ways in which cephalopods

Octopuses are masters at crawling into and through narrow spaces. (top left). Movement, prey manipulation, cleaning, smelling and exploring by touch are all performed by dozens of suckers along the arms (top right). This octopus crawls along the bottom using sinuous movements of its arms and many grasping suckers (bottom).

Octopuses are skilled at searching the seafloor for food in a range of sizes.

hunt and gather food. Octopuses may actively scour a sandy bottom to flush out small prey, or crawl in and over rocky areas to hunt crabs and shrimps. Some larger octopuses will pounce on a large rock and cover it with their arm web. Then they'll roll the rock over and eat whatever is hiding underneath. Octopuses can also use their ability to match their background color and texture while waiting silently for unsuspecting animals to come near.

Octopuses may eat their prey where they kill it, but often they drag it back to their den. Octopus dens may be a crack between some rocks, an empty shell or a sandy depression. Marine biologists studying reef octopuses often find the dens by looking for middens, which are piles of discarded shells and debris just outside the den.

Shrimps, crabs and other crustaceans are a favorite food of octopuses. After breaking the shell with its beak or scraping the shell with its radula, the octopus ejects poison into the prey. Octopuses

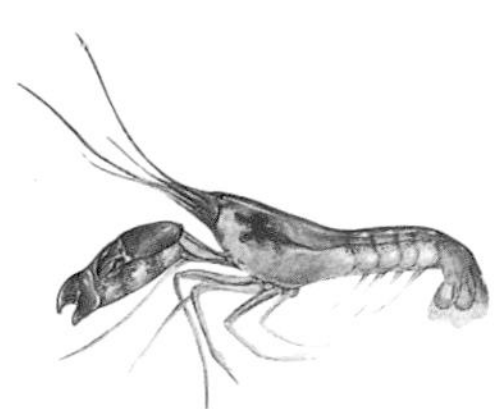

Snapping shrimp

An octopus dines in its den, relatively safe from its own predators (bottom).

also may inject a kind of chemical, which specifically targets the muscle attachment sites of crabs and other crustaceans. The muscles fall cleanly away from the inside of the shell, letting the octopus dine on all of the meat. Discarded crab shells often appear in middens as nearly perfect hollow crabs with a single hole in the carapace.

The typical octopuses most people know all belong to a group called the Incirrata, or incirrate octopuses. There is another group of octopuses, which relatively few people are aware of, and fewer still have seen alive. These are the Cirrata, or cirrate octopuses. Cirrate octopuses are the deep sea specialists of the octopus group. They have eight arms, two eyes, a head, mantle, and siphon like the incirrates, but they also have webbing which extends far along the arms and creates a bell shape. They also have a pair of fins like their relatives, the squids.

Resting along a sandy depression on the ocean floor sits the flapjack devilfish *(Opisthoteuthis)*. Looking like little more than an orange lump, it appears somewhat like a jellyfish. Then it moves. Flapping its fins, it lifts a few feet above the seafloor and glides along with the current. It spreads out the webbing between its arms and hovers like an orange umbrella with bright black eyes. Soon, it settles again to the bottom, curls its arms delicately around itself, and waits.

Cirrates of the deep ocean floor use their fins to swim off the bottom and then drift with bottom currents in search of food or a safe place to settle. Little is known about their eating habits and reproduction but laboratory observations suggest that they eat tiny prey in their natural environment.

Cirrate octopuses like the flapjack devilfish are named for rows of thin sensory organs called cirri which run along the arms with the suckers. Recently, scientists learned of one adaptive function of the cirri in these octopuses by using remotely operated vehicles, (ROVs). The cirri of the Dumbo octopus *(Grimpoteuthis)* were observed to be used during feeding. They beat in rows and direct food toward the

Powerful crab claws are no match for an octopus, which deftly maneuvers over the crab before injecting poison into it, immobilizing it within seconds so it can eat it without harm (top). Cirrate octopuses have cirri, which can be used in feeding (middle and bottom).

mouth of the octopus. Because cirrate octopuses live along the bottom of the sea, scientists think that they use their cirri to hunt for small worms and shellfish, which live in swarms near the bottom.

A cirrate octopus uses the webbing between its arms to trap a swarm of tiny animals and uses the cirri to direct the swarm towards the mouth. Or it may rest quietly on the seafloor and use currents generated by beating cirri to draw individual prey under its arm web and towards its mouth. It has also been suggested that cirri are used to flush tiny prey out of the seafloor.

This octopus is nicknamed "Dumbo" because it's often seen "flying" through the water by flapping its "ears," which are actually fins.

Squids Slick and speedy, their torpedo-shaped bodies rocket through the water. Whereas octopuses have developed a bottom-dwelling lifestyle, squids are specialists in the open sea. Like octopuses, squids draw water into their mantle cavity and over their gills for respiration. They have torpedo-shaped bodies and two fins that are used for steering and swimming. Squids are very energetic swimmers and regularly use jet propulsion for cruising as well as escaping from predators in a cloud of ink. Squids have eight arms, but they also have two longer head appendages called tentacles. The tentacles are specialized for capturing prey in the open ocean. The edges of the suckers along the tentacles are lined with a hardened material called chitin, similar to our fingernails. The chitinous rings are shaped like "teeth," which can grasp an animal once the sucker touches it.

In some squids, the chitinous rings are shaped like claws and are called hooks. Hooks are found at the tips of the tentacles, where the

Colorful streaks are displayed by squids, like this Caribbean reef squid (middle) and market squid (bottom).

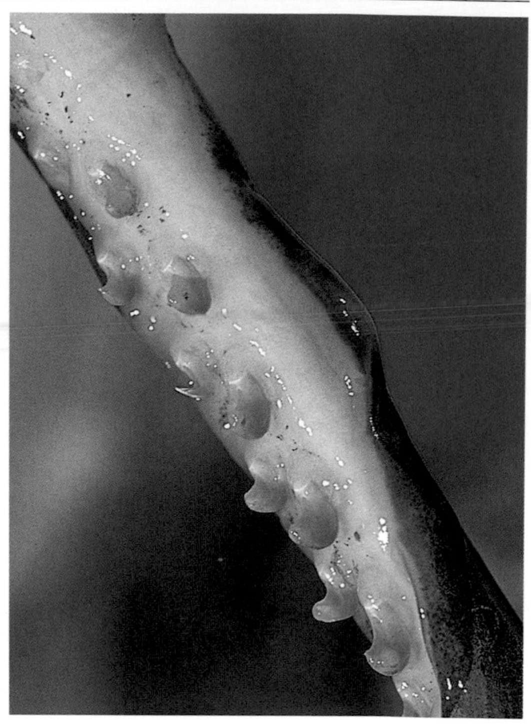

tentacle widens into the club. Typically, squids hunt other animals in the three-dimensional space of the open sea where there are no walls or other hard objects against which to trap prey. The tentacles have a different muscle structure than the arms that allows the tentacles to stretch out very long and then recoil, much like rubber bands.

Squids face their prey, moving silently and deftly forward. The arms curl back around the head as the squid prepares to attack. At a distance usually greater than the length of the squid itself, the attack begins. The tentacles are thrust forward and the clubs strike the prey, sometimes pushing it away just a little. But as the tentacles recoil, the hooks on the clubs pierce the flesh and drag it back towards the eight waiting arms. The arms seize the prey with their chitinous rings and the food is turned quickly to the mouth. If the prey is a fish, the spine will be severed. If the squid has caught a shrimp, the shell will be broken. In either case, the squid injects poison then eats the animal.

Within the arms of squids are a special pair of appendages called tentacles (top left). Squid tentacles are often armed with hooks, which are themselves modified suckers (top right).

Some squids conceal themselves by burying themselves in the sand, like this squid awaiting prey (bottom).

Cuttlefishes Cuttlefishes also have eight arms and two tentacles and are grouped together with the squids as decapods or "ten-footed" cephalopods. There are several important differences between cuttlefishes and squids. The arms and tentacles of cuttlefishes do not have hooks. The fins of cuttlefishes are very delicate and run completely around the edge of the body. Finally, while the skeleton of squids is thin and made from chitin, the skeleton of a cuttlefish is a porous oval calcium "bone," or cuttlebone. You may have seen cuttlebones for sale in pet shops. Bird owners give cuttlebones to their pets as a toy, which keeps beaks sharp and healthy, and provides calcium for their diet.

Cuttlefishes usually live in relatively shallow seas, hovering a few feet above the seafloor. They swim continually like most squids, but are still associated with the bottom for food and protection. Cuttlefishes hunt for bottom-dwelling crabs and shrimps using their tentacles in much the same way that squids hunt. They lack hooks, however, since cuttlefishes can use the bottom to help trap prey.

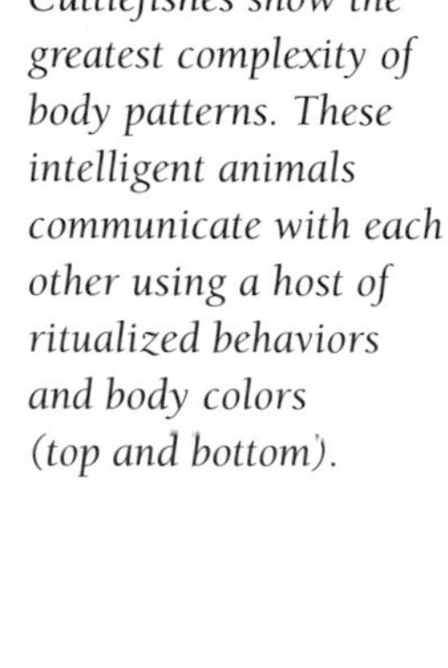

Cuttlefishes show the greatest complexity of body patterns. These intelligent animals communicate with each other using a host of ritualized behaviors and body colors (top and bottom).

Cuttlefishes use a wide variety of color patterns and behaviors to communicate with one another. Stripes and patches of color combine with twisting arms and quick movements to convey threats

or courtship displays. During mating season, a male cuttlefish may display a calming courtship display to a female on one side of its body while flashing a strong warning display to a rival male on the other side of its body. This kind of control and communication is incredible to watch, making cuttlefishes popular animals among marine behaviorists.

One of the most widely studied cuttlefishes is *Sepia officianalis*. This species is found in relatively shallow waters of the Atlantic Ocean along Europe and Africa. The name *sepia* refers to the deep-brown ink, which was prized throughout Europe by artists. Over sandy stretches of the Mediterranean Sea, cuttlefishes often hover a few inches off the bottom. With steady pulses from their siphons, they scour the seafloor, flushing out shrimps or crabs that are buried near the surface. When found, the prey are quickly pinned by the tentacle clubs and drawn up to the sharp beak of the cuttlefish.

Successful males court females and transfer sperm to them by using a special arm (top left). Rival male cuttlefishes sometimes fight for access to females during mating season (top right).

Curious cuttlefish will often hover a few feet from divers, allowing their pictures to be taken (bottom).

ROV Submersibles

The R/V Point Lobos *(top) sails into the bay to deploy the ROV,* Ventana *(bottom).*

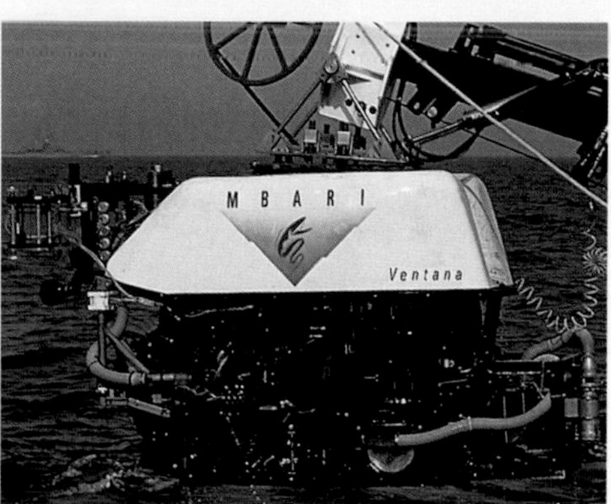

The use of mechanical underwater robots is allowing biological oceanographers to study the behavior and ecology of deep sea animals for the first time. Researchers at the Monterey Bay Aquarium Research Institute (MBARI) use a submersible called a remotely operated vehicle or ROV to study the deep ocean life in Monterey Bay, California. The ROV is named the *Ventana,* which is the Spanish word for "window." While traditional oceanographic surveys have revealed much about life in the deep sea, ROV surveys provide the only direct observations of deep sea animals. Furthermore, ROVs can gently collect live specimens in pristine condition for further laboratory observations or exhibit in public aquariums. ROV and laboratory observations yield valuable insights into the behavior of deep sea jellies, worms, shrimp, fishes and cephalopods.

The *Ventana* can dive to depths of about one mile. In 1996, MBARI developed and designed a new ROV, the *Tiburon,* which is Spanish for "shark." The *Tiburon* can dive to depths of over 13,000 feet or 2.5 miles to reach the deepest part of the Monterey Canyon. The deepest water in the world is a little more than six miles in the Mariana Trench south of Japan and east of the Philippines. The Japan Marine Science and Technology Center (JAMSTEC) has an ROV capable of exploring these extreme depths. This ROV is called the *Kaiko,* which is the Japanese word for "trench."

Not all research submersibles are remotely operated. Some are operated by human pilots. In the United States, the most notable crewed submersibles are the Johnson Sealinks I and II—each using a Plexiglas sphere for housing the pilot and scientist, and capable of 3,000-foot dives. The Alvin uses a metal sphere and can dive to over 13,000 feet. The deepest diving crewed submersible is the Shinkai 6,500, which translates from Japanese as "The Deep-Sea 6,500 meters" because it can dive to that depth, (over 21,000 feet).

Submersibles are being used to explore the biology, geology, chemistry and physical oceanography of the world's deep oceans. Information obtained through submersible research is beginning to shed light on the mysteries of a dark world and its eerie inhabitants.

A vampire squid glides swiftly through the water by beating its large fins. Rediscovered in 1903, this animal is the only member of an ancient group thought to have gone extinct.

Before attack, a cuttlefish sends rippling waves of color across its body, which sometimes appear to us as the shadows of waves. Just how these patterns lull potential prey is still unclear.

Vampire Squid *Vampyroteuthis* is a living fossil that is not really a squid, cuttlefish or octopus, but it possesses some features of each of these groups.

Vampyroteuthis has eight arms like an octopus and so is sometimes grouped with octopuses as octopods or "eight-footed" cephalopods, but it also has two additional appendages called filaments. These filaments are unlike the tentacles in squids and cuttlefishes and are unique to vampire squid. *Vampyroteuthis* lives in the deep open ocean and has a lifestyle similar to squids. Yet the part of the brain sensitive to touch is well developed as it is in octopuses.

Vampyroteuthis has fins, cirri and a web connecting the arms and so was originally classified as a cirrate octopus. But research pioneered by Dr. Grace Pickford in the 1940s and 1950s showed that *Vampyroteuthis* was truly unique among the world's living creatures. Cephalopod paleontologists have shown that *Vampyroteuthis* is most likely a modern representative of a group of cephalopods thought to have gone extinct around the time of the dinosaurs.

Coleoids Octopuses, squids, cuttlefishes and vampire squid together make up a group of cephalopods called coleoids. These animals have evolved from ancestors, which originally had an external shell for protection. Over time, the shell in coleoids moved inside the animal as a skeleton and changed in many ways. In squids, the shell became a thin, flexible rod along the back called a pen. The pen, like the beak and hooks, is made of chitin. In cuttlefishes, the skeleton is made of calcium and is full of tiny holes. These holes are used to hold varying amounts of gas to control the buoyancy of the cuttlefish. The skeleton of *Vampyroteuthis* is similar to a squid pen, but the shape is reminiscent of fossil cephalopod pens. The skeleton of octopuses has been lost completely since they do not need a skeleton for buoyancy. This also allows them to squeeze through the small cracks and holes.

Nautiloids The other group of living cephalopods are the nautiloids, which are represented by only one genus, the chambered nautilus (*Nautilus* sp.). The nautilus is prized for its beautiful shell, which is often polished and sold in tourist shops where tropical shells are common. Nautiluses have several dozen arms and no tentacles. There are no suckers on their arms. Their two eyes are much less developed than coleoid eyes and have often been compared to a pinhole camera.

The shell of the nautilus coils in on itself in graceful whirls. Inside the calcium shell many walls, or septa divide the shell into chambers. The animal lives in the last chamber and creates new, larger chambers as it grows. Through all the chambers runs one single organ called a siphuncle. This tissue pumps fluids into and out of the chambers of the nautilus shell. Depending on the amount of gas in the chambers, the nautilus will rise or sink in the water. The nautilus uses this system to control its buoyancy.

Ammonites The nautilus is the only living cephalopod with an external shell, but many ancient cephalopods relied on external shells for survival, including ammonites, a large and diverse group of shelled cephalopods. Fossil ammonite shells are prized by collectors and provided paleontologists with a fairly good record of cephalopod evolution.

The shell of the ammonite coiled around like a nautilus' shell, but there are many differences. Ammonites shells were sometimes huge, measuring over six feet in diameter. The great size and weight of such a shell was supported by complex septa, which left beautifully etched patterns on many fossils. The difference in septa patterns is one of the key features used by paleontologists to trace the evolution of the group.

Ammonites became extinct about the same time as dinosaurs. They were an enormously successful group until that time and it is still a mystery as to why they suddenly went extinct. Was their fate linked to dinosaurs? Nobody is certain, but research on the extinction of ammonites has fueled some debate about extinction in general and of dinosaurs in particular.

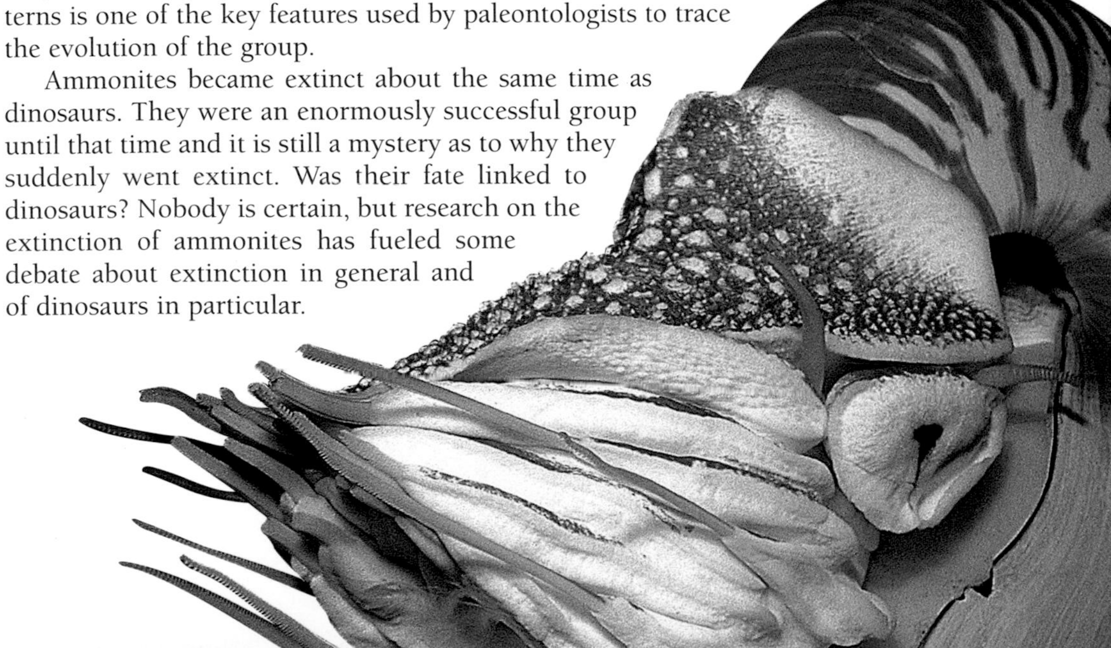

One of the oldest lineages of cephalopods is the nautiloids, with their numerous arms, primitive eyes, and hard outer shell often prized by collectors and tourists.

3

Courtship and Mating

On a clear and cool autumn night in Monterey, California, there is a peace and tranquillity that blankets the bay. The night breeze carries the scent of rocky beaches and algae as I look out over the water, black as pitch. I have often sat at night along the shore of Monterey and marveled at the tremendous size of the submarine canyon hidden from view by the waters of the bay. Comparable in size to the Grand Canyon in the southwestern United States, the Monterey Canyon reaches a depth of over 14,000 feet as it meanders seaward.

At night, the bay may look still and quiet from shore, but beneath the surface life continues to turn its cycle. In my mind's eye, I can see the hosts of creatures, which live deep in the bay during the day, out of the reach of sunlight, now rising to the surface to hunt and eat. I look down at the waves breaking along the shore and imagine those species of octopuses, crabs and fishes,

Monterey Bay is the scene of seasonal squid orgies (bottom).

which only hunt at night, coming out of their hiding places and beginning to move about in search of food.

This duality of the night sea has always intrigued me. It appears so still and serene yet I know that beneath this calmness there are countless millions of animals interacting with each other. The activity may change with the hour or the season depending on, which species are migrating through. But autumn is the breeding season of the market squid *(Loligo opalescens)* and all around the bay I can imagine them gathering as similar species do in bays in Peru, Nova Scotia, Japan, Polynesia, India, Madagascar, Brazil and Spain. From the Gulf of Mexico to the Gulf of Thailand, market squid gather and support commercial fisheries throughout the world. Soon the full moon will rise over the mountains to the east and the market squid will come to the surface to court and reproduce as they have for thousands of years.

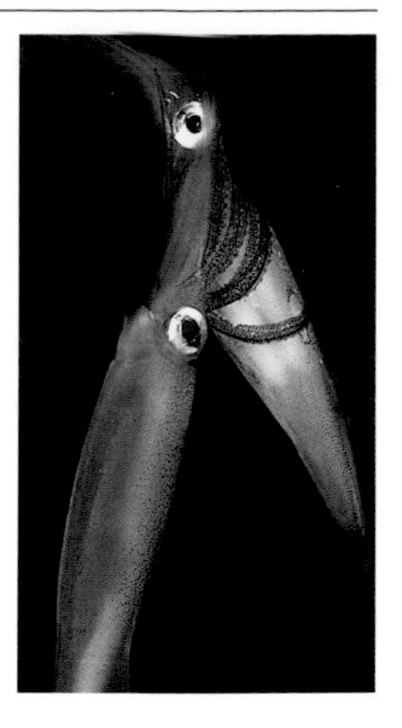

A pair of squid entwine in a mating embrace. The male will transfer packets of sperm to the female using his hectocotylus arm (top).

Schools of squid gather under the light of the moon near the surface of Monterey Bay to mate. Schools of similar-sized adults actively swim together during this season. We don't know what triggers the orgy, but as soon as a few individuals begin mating and laying eggs, all others in the mating schools quickly join in.

Males become highly excited and begin darting around, occasionally ejecting ink. They may bump into other males and flash warning colors or threaten them by curling some of their arms. It is unusual for males to actually grasp and bite each other, but it happens. Females also dart energetically through the water, flashing colorful signals to males about their willingness to mate.

Flashes of color, quick bursts of speed and trails of ink abound within a mating school of squid.

Once a male finds a female suitable for mating, he will try to swim between her and rival males within the group. If another male approaches, the guarding male will warn him to stay away by aggressively signaling or even charging him. If the intruding male does not leave, the two may fight. The victor then escorts the female.

The male approaches the female carefully at first, sometimes gliding a single arm along her mantle and stroking her. He may demonstrate readiness to mate by creating a colorful patch along his back over his reproductive organs. If she accepts him, he will swim beneath her and grasp her with his eight arms near the opening of the mantle. His arms become dark maroon as her body becomes pale white in sharp contrast. With one quick movement he reaches one specialized arm into his mantle cavity and grabs a packet of sperm, which he transfers to the female.

This arm has been shaped for holding and transferring sperm packets and is called a hectocotylus. The name comes from biologist George Cuvier who found the broken tips of the arms within female cephalopods and mistakenly thought they were parasitic worms, which he called hectocotylus. The hectocotylus arm grabs several packets of sperm ejected from the penis and reaches into the female's mantle cavity to place them near her oviduct.

The pair then break apart but remain swimming together while the female prepares to lay some eggs. She uses many specialized organs in her body to carefully wrap the eggs in protective jelly. The eggs are then bound into an egg case, each containing about 200 or so fertilized eggs. The egg case is ejected and the female uses her arms to firmly cement the egg case to rocks or to some other suitable surface such as algae on the seafloor. She may cement her eggs to other egg cases already laid by other females in the group.

The mating pair continues to reproduce and lay eggs in several bouts of mating. Cephalopods generally die after mating. This rule will probably prove to have exceptions as we learn more about the mating habits of little-known cephalopods, especially the deep sea

octopuses and squids. Market squid, however, do abide by this rule and die soon after mating is completed. Spent males drift to the seafloor and die. Females attach their final egg cases in place, and having finished that final task, die as well. The resulting scene is unnerving and somewhat empty. One generation of squid lies dead among the waving fingers of egg cases housing the next generation. It is as if the squid cease to exist, leaving only the hope of vast numbers of developing eggs, which will hatch and grow in the open sea to someday return and create this eerie interlude once again.

The egg cases may cover an area of seafloor farther than the eye can see with thousands upon thousands of egg cases, each holding hundreds of developing eggs. In about a month, the hatchlings will push their way free of the eggs and begin darting about in quick little jerks created from great pushes of water through their siphons. They are no bigger than a single grain of rice and a great majority of the newly hatched young will never return to this place to breed. Instead they will end up in the hungry mouths of fishes, marine mammals, birds and a host of invertebrate animals.

But some of these rice-sized squid will grow and mature in the open ocean. No one is exactly sure where they go. We know about the early development of squids and about their adult reproductive behavior, but we know little about what occurs in between. All we know for certain is that each year a new group of mature *Loligo* enter Monterey Bay and other bays all over the world to court under the moonlight filtering through the ocean surface.

The Jig is Up During the squid's riotous mating ritual, moonlight will not be the only light on the bay. Near midnight, squid-fishing boats sail out of Monterey Harbor and prepare to go to work. During the early morning hours, each boat will shine a battery of lights over the bay. Some times you can see more than a dozen ships lined around the edge of the bay, their lights glistening off the water.

Monterey has been renowned as a fishing community for decades. Throughout the middle of the twentieth century, the sardine fisheries

When mating is finished, the adult squid die (top). After mating, the female squid attaches her eggs to the seafloor or to other cases (middle). Squid have provided a great commercial food source for people all over the world (bottom).

supported more than a dozen major commercial canneries and inspired novelist John Steinbeck to write *Cannery Row.* Today, the bay supports an active commercial squid-fishing industry. The common market squid is harvested annually and supplies much of the western United States and Canada with fresh calamari.

In the past, traditional squid-fishing boats called "jiggers" used an array of bright lights to attract schools of squid. The fishermen then used special lures called jigs, which are bounced up and down in the water, a motion that causes a squid to attack the lure and become caught. Today jiggers are being replaced by more efficient net seiner ships, although in many areas around the world, squid jigging is still common. Market squid are very meaty animals and little of the commercial catch is wasted. The few parts of the animals not used for human consumption are returned to the sea and make a meal for seabirds and surface-dwelling fishes.

Squid are also an important prey for many marine birds, like this Heermann's gull.

The Not-So-Cuddly Cuttle Off the southern coast of Australia resides the world's largest cuttlefish, *Sepia apama.* This beautiful and colorful animal can reach lengths of three feet or more. Often curious, this cuttlefish will allow divers to approach slowly as it flashes a wondrous variety of color patterns, from yellow to brilliant green, with flecks of white and brown along the body. But this cuttlefish has been known to bite divers who get too close.

During mating season, male cuttlefishes will also occasionally bite each other while fighting for choice mating dens. Contests between rival males usually end without injury as one male gives way to the threats of another. But some males have been seen with arms missing or with deep wounds in their backs from fights during mating season.

The large Sepia apama *cuttlefish is a popular attraction for Australian divers, but must be treated with respect.*

Cuttlefish eggs hang from the roof of this den. Within a few weeks to months, a fully formed hatchling will emerge from each egg and begin darting around in search of food.

Female cuttlefishes soon appear at the dens and mate with the resident males. After mating, the female retreats deep within the den to lay her eggs one at a time. She coats each egg with a protective sheath and carefully cements it to the roof of the den. She will leave the eggs unattended to develop and hatch on their own.

The Brooding Octopus While diving off the coast of St. Croix in the Caribbean Sea, I came across an unusual sight. A clamshell snapped closed upon my approach, but through the tiny crack I saw what appeared to be suckers. I hid behind a coral head to get a better look. After a few minutes, the shell cracked opened. A few arms tentatively felt around the outer rim of the shell, then it opened completely and I saw a dwarf octopus *(Octopus joubini)* inside. Although she was no more than an inch long, she was obviously a fully mature female because inside the shell were hundreds of developing eggs. She would clean and aerate the eggs by gently blowing water across them and stroking them with her arms.

The general mating habits of incirrate octopuses have been known for many years, based on research conducted on the reproductive behavior of the common octopus *(Octopus vulgaris)*. Observations of the North Pacific giant octopus *(Octopus dofleini)* and the common red octopus *(Octopus rubescens)* of western North America support the general trend for incirrate octopuses. Details for each species may differ and virtually nothing is known about the reproductive behavior of the deep sea cirrate octopuses.

While the market squid schools, most octopuses typically live solitary lives along the bottom. They find or create a den for

Dwarf octopuses are very difficult for divers to find, since they are only an inch long.

themselves and go about the business of daily life quite apart from other octopuses. During the breeding season, octopuses may roam farther away from their home sites on the chance of meeting a suitable partner for mating.

When two octopuses meet during mating season, they flash color signals to one another. Males often show enlarged suckers in the middle of their arms to a potential partner. Perhaps they can determine the sex of the other using this display of suckers.

For red octopuses, courtship continues for hours. A male silently approaches a female, flashing color patterns and darkening his eyes. He may tenuously reach an arm out to the female and stroke her. If she accepts him, mating will begin and may last from 20 minutes to over an hour.

The red octopus is common along the coasts of western North America (top). Two octopuses engage in mating behavior (bottom).

The male uses his hectocotylus arm to transfer sperm to the female. The female then accepts the package and keeps it for later use. She will soon leave the male and return to her den to lay fertilized eggs. Scientists believe she will mate only once before laying eggs. The male, in contrast, may continue the search for another partner throughout the breeding season before he dies.

Back at her den, the female lays thousands of eggs in long strings, which she attaches to the roof of her lair. The strings of developing eggs hang all around her and she gently pulses water from her siphon to aerate the eggs and clean debris from the strands.

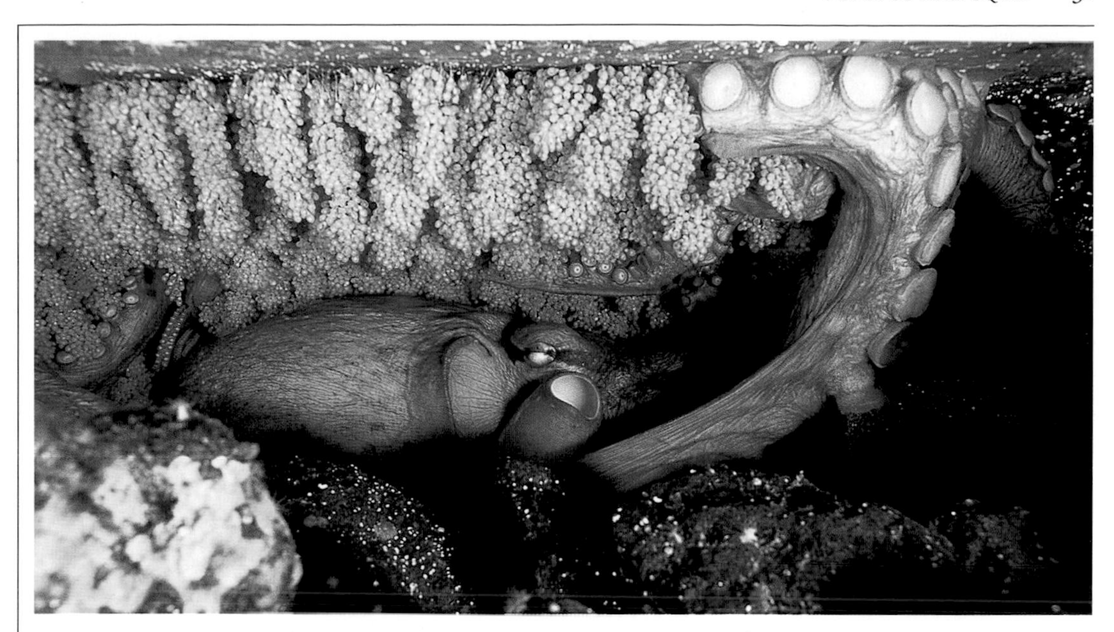

She will continue to care for the eggs in this way for several weeks to several months, depending on the species. She will only leave her den to fend off would-be scavengers looking for an easy meal of octopus eggs. She will not eat during the entire incubation period and refuses food even when offered by researchers or recreational scuba divers.

Divers have tried to entice brooding octopuses to feed by holding tasty bits of shrimp or fish right next to the mouth, only to be ignored or even attacked. It seems the biology of the octopus at this point relegates her to being interested only in protecting her young until they hatch. After the hatchlings are free, the mother, having finished her final task in life, dies.

As with squids, little is known about the natural ecology of octopus hatchlings. Recent work has shown that they often find their way into the pelagic food web as part of the plankton or micronekton. How these animals are distributed and where they settle out of the plankton is one source of current investigation into the life cycles of cephalopods.

Filling in the Holes with Submersible Science Recent submersible observations by the ROV *Ventana* (see page 21) provide another clue to the life cycle of the red octopus. During the summer months in Monterey, groups of schooling red octopus were recorded in the uppermost 1,300 feet of water. This was the first direct evidence that octopuses schooled like their cousins the squids. All of the individuals within the school were about the same size, from one to two inches in length. Schools of more than 50 animals were observed in the lights of the submersible.

It is still unclear at what size or age an individual red octopus settles to the seafloor and begins life on the bottom. However, these schools were rarely observed during the winter months and individuals collected by the submersible easily adapted to a bottom-dwelling

In lairs, female octopuses defend their developing eggs (top) until they hatch (middle), sometimes wrapping their arms around the brood (bottom).

Although most octopuses live along the seafloor and have muscular bodies (top), some octopuses have become gelatinous and live out in the open ocean (bottom).

life in laboratory aquaria. This suggests that the octopuses may be settling out soon after the summer schooling season. One way to test this theory would be to compare the age of schooling octopuses to the age of "adult" octopuses found along the floor of the Monterey Canyon.

You can tell the age of a cephalopod by closely examining calcium balls called statoliths, which the animal uses for balance. The cephalopod lays down a ring of calcium each day. By cutting a thin cross-section through a statolith, you can count the daily growth rings in much the same way you can count the annual growth rings in a tree trunk.

A Chance Encounter The ROV *Ventana* also provided information about the reproduction of a different kind of deep sea octopus, called *Bolitaena. Bolitaena* is an exception among octopuses because it lives in the deep open ocean, away from the bottom. This incirrate octopus is very gelatinous and nearly transparent. You can see its gills and other internal organs through the mantle, much like you can see inside a jelly.

While conducting an ROV survey of the deep sea life in Monterey Bay, the ROV happened upon a single female

Bolitaena. She held thousands of tiny developing eggs inside her arms! She was brooding them like her bottom-dwelling cousins, although she was doing so in the middle of the open ocean. A slit along the webbing between the arms closest to the siphon allowed the siphon to gently blow water across the eggs for aeration. Close inspection revealed tiny pairs of eyes within each egg and that each egg was attached to others, similar to eggs in a bottom-dwelling octopus' lair. The internal organs of the mother were almost gone and a skin had formed across her mouth. It appeared that she, too, would die after the eggs were hatched.

This kind of behavior had never been directly observed before in such an octopus. It demonstrates how a single animal observed from a submersible can tell us volumes about the lives of little-known deep sea animals.

The event also illustrates the cooperation among the world's leading marine research institutions and aquariums in an effort to increase both scientific understanding and public appreciation of the wonderful diversity of marine animals on our planet. MBARI scientists worked closely with scientists and aquaculturists from the Monterey Bay Aquarium to share resources and information about *Bolitaena.* This kind of effort leads to more efficient study of marine animals and will allow greater public access to strange and novel marine life as we learn more about how to provide for them in aquaria and how to care for the young.

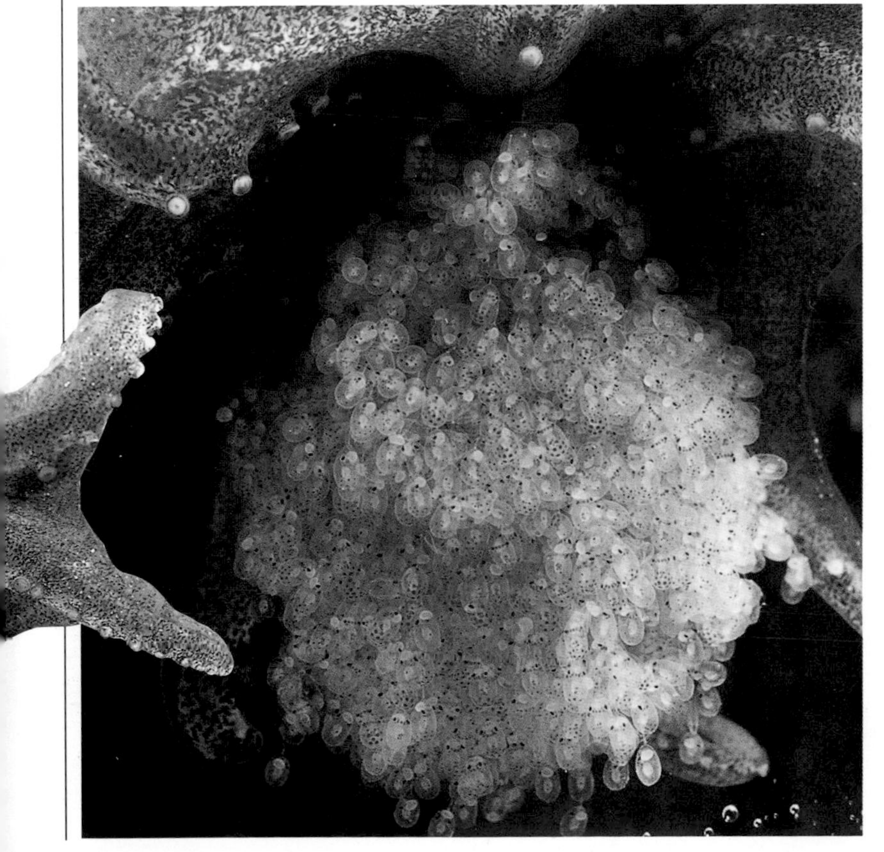

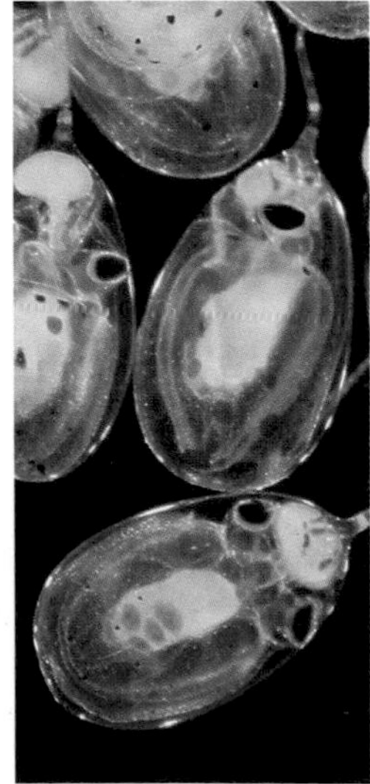

A recent discovery shows that open ocean gelatinous octopuses brood developing eggs within their arms (bottom left). Each egg contains a single developing octopus (bottom right).

Fisheries and Marine Ecology

Fishermen provide valuable information for biologists as well as a valuable food source for people.

Commercial fishermen and marine ecologists have two very important things in common: both rely on the sea and its rich fauna for their livelihood and both have a critical interest in preserving the natural balance of our oceans. Historically, disagreements have arisen between the two groups as many marine ecologists blamed commercial fishermen for exploiting certain marine resources to a level harmful to the overall ecology of the oceans, while some commercial fishermen accused marine ecologists of interfering with their business and being unconcerned about the livelihood of the fishermen. In hindsight, perhaps both of these accusations were true in some cases.

Today however, most ecologists and fishermen have come to understand that each is critical to the other. Information provided by commercial fishermen is pivotal to marine ecologists trying to understand the fluctuations of marine populations in a given area. There are often too few marine ecologists to sample an area. Conversely, the more information marine ecologists have, the better able they are to provide the fishing industry with information about the amounts, which can be safely harvested while allowing marine populations to maintain a stable, sustainable yield each year. This allows commercial fisheries to continue to operate and predict their catches and provides people with a valuable food source. Too often we forget that ecology includes the interactions of all species—including our own. Human consumption must fit into the scheme of nature along with that of other top predators like sharks, seals or whales.

Collapse of the once-flourishing sardine industry in Monterey Bay clearly demonstrated the need for fisherman and marine ecologists to work together. Today, they are cooperating so the valuable market squid fishery will be managed in a sustainable manner. Globally, problems persist: all but two of the world's 15 major fishing areas are fished at or beyond sustainable capacity.

4

Escape Artists

Of all the world's animals, cephalopods have one of the most diverse arsenals of defenses at their disposal. They can change their appearance in the blink of an eye to blend with the background, or disappear in a cloud of ink. Some live in shells, and others are deadly poisonous. Some cephalopods even produce their own light and actually use this light to disappear against a dimly lit background. And there are some species of squid who can "fly!"

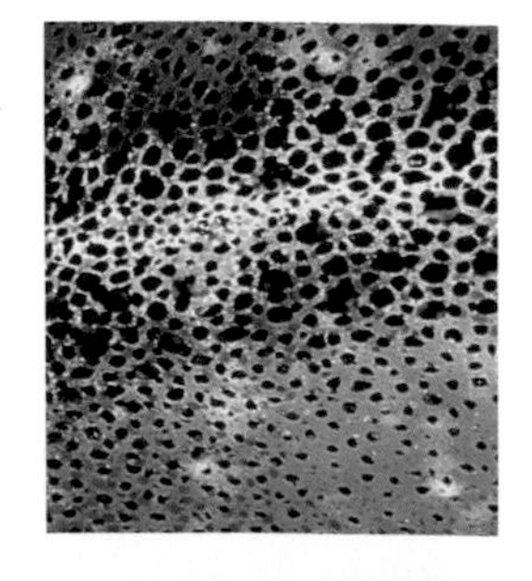

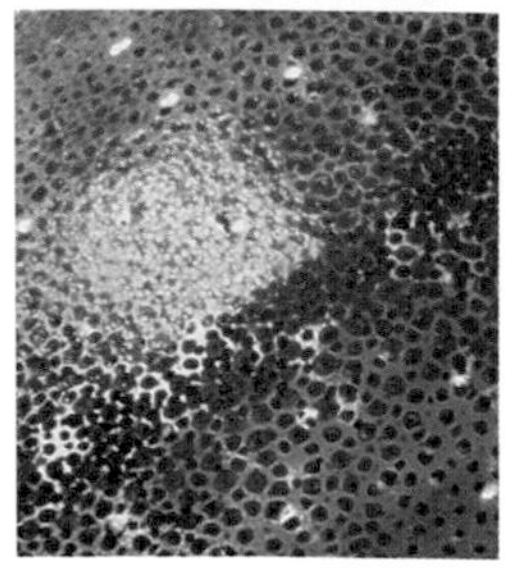

Octopuses excel at hiding either by camouflaging their skin (right), using chromatophores (top) or by tucking into small places (bottom).

Color Changes Cephalopods as a group are known for their ability to change color and eject ink, although not all have these abilities. With the exception of the hard-shelled chambered nautilus, the "paper-shelled" argonaut, and a few species of deep sea scaled squids, all modern cephalopods have soft bodies with smooth, slippery skin exposed directly to the sea. The skin is very delicate and easily damaged. Various cells within the skin combine to control the color and sheen of the cephalopod.

Chromatophores, or color organs, are like sacs of colored pigment that expand or contract in groups to quickly change the color of an entire animal or a section of the animal. When a color organ is relaxed, all the pigment within the cell is concentrated at the center, forming a tiny dot to an observer. If you look closely at the skin of an octopus or a squid, you can see these tiny dots clearly within an area, which appears pale or white. When the color organ is not relaxed, the muscles around the cell stretch and pull it into a flattened disk shape, which spreads out the pigment and colors the area. Color organs are colored by pigments in the melanin family. Melanin is the same type of compound that colors human skin different shades. The concentration of melanin components in a cell gives that cell its color. In cephalopods, these colors are red, orange, yellow, brown or black. Some cephalopods use all these colors and are adept at changing color quickly. Others are only one color and cannot change color at all.

There are also other specialized cells called iridocytes, which act like mirrors or prisms and reflect light at various angles. Cells may reflect all wavelengths of light producing a pure white color. Other cells may refract white light into all the component colors thereby creating brilliant blues, yellows, reds, purples, oranges and greens. The

Cuttlefishes may use colors to blend into the background (top left) or to brilliantly flash and warn other animals to stay away (top right).

iridocytes are usually found below the color organs in a cephalopod's skin, but not always. In some cases, iridocytes are on top of the color organs and create vibrant warning color patterns in poisonous species to advertise their danger to a would-be predator.

One beautiful octopus named *Japetella* lives out in the open ocean and is nearly completely transparent. However, throughout the body and head of *Japetella* are rows and rows of iridocytes, which refract white light into all the vibrant colors of the rainbow. As this octopus spins in the water, it provides a dazzling display, of bright reds, then yellows, greens and blues.

Combined together, all of the chromatophores and iridocytes can quickly change a ruddy-colored octopus to bright orange, or to a red-and-white-striped animal. Squids and cuttlefishes also use color organs to create stripes, spots and other skin patterns over their bodies. These patterns are sometimes used as camouflage, but other times they're used to communicate with other members of their species.

Incirrate octopuses and some cuttlefishes have an additional feature in their skin, which enhances their ability to camouflage themselves. They can change the texture of their skin and actually "sculpt" it to look like the surrounding bottom. Folds of skin called papillae extend from the body. Muscles located around the folds of skin contract or relax, changing the texture or apparent roughness of the skin.

Over a smooth sandy bottom, an octopus may become nearly white with very smooth skin. The same octopus over a coral reef might change its skin color to match the color of the reef, and its skin texture to reflect the bumpiness of the coral. Stories of the abilities of reef octopuses to camouflage themselves are often exaggerated, but the truth is still astounding. Tiny reef octopuses will attempt to mimic everything from a purple snail shell to a red-and-white bottlecap with great success.

Octopuses not only match the color of the background, but also match their overall scheme of colors and textures of their habitat, such as this reef octopus mimicking a sponge (left).

Inking The ability of most cephalopods to eject a blob of ink is well known. The inks range in color from light brown to deep black. The color is created by melanin pigments suspended in a clear fluid. Ink is stored in a sac inside the squid or octopus and is released through the funnel when needed.

Sometimes the ink cloud is shaped like the body of the animal that released it, and is a pseudomorph, or "false body." The false body may fool a potential predator into attacking it rather than the animal. If the predator falls for it, the cephalopod can escape. After inking, an octopus or squid often flushes to a light color (in contrast to the dark ink), changes its course and rapidly jets away.

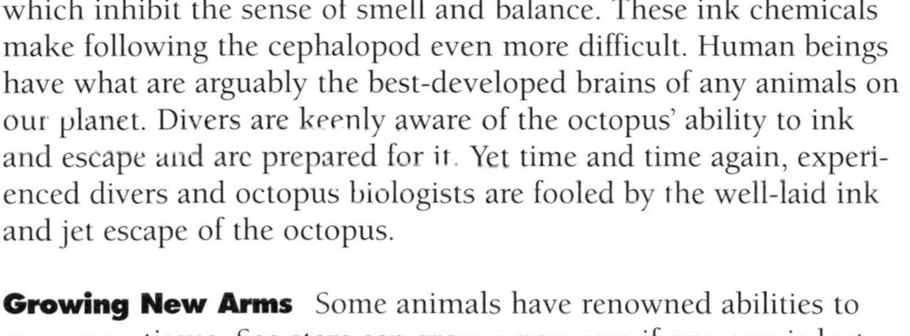

The ink contains an eye irritant (tyrosinase) and other chemicals which inhibit the sense of smell and balance. These ink chemicals make following the cephalopod even more difficult. Human beings have what are arguably the best-developed brains of any animals on our planet. Divers are keenly aware of the octopus' ability to ink and escape and are prepared for it. Yet time and time again, experienced divers and octopus biologists are fooled by the well-laid ink and jet escape of the octopus.

When threatened, octopuses will release a cloud of ink as they jet away from danger (left and top).

Growing New Arms Some animals have renowned abilities to grow new tissue. Sea stars can grow a new arm if one arm is lost. Some worms can grow new segments if old ones are lost or severed. Other animals purposefully break off or autotomize parts of their bodies as a defensive tactic. Some lizards break off their tails and leave the tail writhing in the sand to distract a predator. Once distracted, the lizard can escape to safety where it will grow a new tail. Sea cucumbers eviscerate or eject their guts through their mouths at a predator, which eats the free meal while the sea cucumber retreats to safety.

Octopuses and other cephalopods also have strong regenerative abilities. If an octopus loses an arm to a predator, it can grow a new arm complete with functional suckers to take its place. Some octopuses have been reported to autotomize arms with the intention of distracting a predator in much the same way a lizard breaks off its tail.

Octopuses can also regenerate new arms to replace ones damaged or torn away by predators. Some break off arms to escape.

Poison When all methods of camouflage or evasive maneuvering fail, a cephalopod is still left with a sharp beak and sometimes formidable suckers. The beak can sharply bite at an attacking animal and salivary glands pump poison into the attacker.

As mentioned before, cephalopods often subdue prey with poison. These poisons, however, may also inflict serious pain or even death on a potential predator. The poisons affect the nerve cells or motor muscles and can stun a fish.

Schooling Although not always thought of as a defense, gathering in large groups of similar size animals, such as a school, provides more protection for a given individual than being alone. Schooling acts to confuse a predator.

Since the individuals within the school look alike and are about the same size, rapid polarized changes in direction can make it difficult to follow any one individual. The next time you visit an aquarium or see a school of fish along the beach, try to follow just one individual with your eyes when the group is moving. It can be very frustrating. If a predator cannot concentrate on any single animal, it makes hunting more difficult and provides the prey a chance for escape.

The common market squid not only breeds in vast schools but probably travels in schools most of its life. Schooling has also been observed in many other squids, and we now know some octopuses (such as the red octopus) also school during part of their lives.

Although not always thought of as a defense, schooling does provide cover for an individual in the frenzied blur of the crowd (left and top). A hard outer shell provides sturdy armor for the tank-like nautilus (bottom). Other cephalopod groups evolved internal shells to allow for greater speed and flexibility.

Novelties Many of the defenses of cephalopods rank among the more unusual in the animal world. Inking, rapid color changes, breaking off an arm, are all fairly novel ways to avoid being eaten. Only cephalopods are adept at so many unusual defenses. Not all cephalopod defenses are novel however.

The external shell of the nautilus, for example, is certainly a tried-and-true defense mechanism used by other molluscs such as snails and clams. The shell of the nautilus does have depth limits (of about 2,000 feet or so), but the extremely long fossil record of nautiloid shells extending back well before dinosaurs or even fishes is testament to the benefit of such armor.

Perhaps the most intriguing cephalopod defense is that of the flying squids from the family Ommastrephidae. These squids also school and when chased to the surface of the sea, they will blast up through the surface with one gigantic push from their siphon. But besides jumping out of the water, they spread out delicate fins and folds of tissue to glide above the water. The neon flying squid, *Ommastrephes bartrami,* has been reported to glide for as much as 60 feet before plunking back down into the water. By this time the predator is baffled and most likely has gone off in another direction. Since the neon flying squid regularly schools, they sometimes jump out of the water and glide in groups of more than 100 animals! I cannot imagine a stranger thing to witness than a "flock" of squid.

When Defenses Fail Despite all the defenses and strategies available to cephalopods, they are still one of the most important prey groups for many predators. Large sharks and fishes routinely hunt squid in the open ocean. Toothed whales and dolphins also feed heavily on cephalopods as do seals and sea lions. Some seabirds gain over half of their diet by taking squids. Finally, many cephalopods will regularly eat other cephalopods.

People have hunted and eaten octopuses and their kin for thousands of years. Octopuses have adorned pottery and ships throughout

Venomous Octopus

Although pretty and tiny, the blue-ringed octopus packs a lethal bite.

Although most octopuses use poison to subdue prey or fend off a predator, only a few species have venom strong enough to be dangerous to humans. One deadly octopus is the blue-ringed octopus *(Hapalochlaena maculosus)*.

Recreational divers and swimmers around Australia's Great Barrier Reef are often warned about contact with the blue-ringed. This tiny reef-dwelling octopus is normally shy and retiring, quite content to escape a diver by retreating quickly into the cracks and crevices of the coral.

Yet when flushed out of hiding, the blue-ringed octopus does not use its skin to blend into the surroundings. Instead it reveals its presence using flashes of color, highlighted by brilliant blue rings throughout the body. Although this display may look very pretty and appealing to us, to many animals this display serves as a bold warning of the potential danger of this animal. Throughout the animal kingdom, poisonous or otherwise unpalatable creatures often "advertise" their defenses with bright colors.

The bright, blue rings of this octopus are created by an arrangement of iridocytes, which lay on top of the color organs directly beneath the skin. The iridocytes are shaped to bend the incoming light so that only blue light is reflected back. The beautiful vibrant blue rings appear to jump right out of the skin.

The venom of the blue-ringed octopus is one of the most deadly poisons known, and makes this species extremely dangerous if not treated with proper respect and care. An individual blue-ringed octopus weighing barely more than an ounce contains enough poison to completely paralyze 10 people weighing 165 pounds each.

As with most other poisonous animals, however, using a little caution and prudence is all that is necessary to avoid any danger when swimming in an area where the blue-ringed octopus lives.

Even with their great arsenal of defenses, cephalopods are eaten by a wide variety of predators including sharks and sea stars

southern Europe and southeast Asia for over four-thousand years. Today, cephalopods are a valued food in countries all over the globe, but particularly in Europe and Africa around the Mediterranean Sea and in far eastern countries such as Japan.

Methods for capturing squids and octopuses often involve jerking lures with many hooks through the water to elicit an attack from the unsuspecting cephalopod. In the case of squids and nocturnal octopuses, lights often lure the animals close to the fishing boats. Fishermen in Hawaii and the Philippines have reportedly used torches for such purposes for hundreds of years.

One unique and intriguing method for fishing cuttlefishes was developed in the Mediterranean Sea. Fishermen there knew that male cuttlefishes would often follow and grab a female cuttlefish. So they captured a live female cuttlefish and towed her behind the boat. When a male grabbed onto the female, the pair was hauled into the boat, the male was removed and the female was cast again to catch another male.

Sometimes octopuses are caught simply by lowering pots and jars into the water. Curious, they will crawl into the pot to explore it. When they do, the fishermen reel in the pot and the octopus within.

The octopus' habit of grabbing items and not letting go has been used by people in other ways in the Far East. To collect items lost on sunken boats, an octopus would be attached to a line and lowered to the sunken boat, where it would grasp an object and, as the line was reeled in, carry it to the surface.

5

Vampires and Giants of the Deep

Much of what we know about our oceans has come from observations of species living in relatively shallow waters and often close to shore. These species are the most readily accessible to divers, commercial fishermen and scientists. Comparatively little is known about the world's deep oceans or the inhabitants of this dark realm.

On August 11, 1930, an intrepid pioneer name William Beebe crammed his six-foot body into a metal ball only four feet in diameter, and was lowered 2,510 feet into the sea. This ball is known as the Bathysphere and Beebe became the first modern deep sea naturalist. His work was to receive much acclaim and attention not only for the very real danger and human intrigue of his quest to explore the unknown depths, but also for his fantastic drawings of the life he observed below. Beebe drew creatures, which looked as though they had come straight from the mind of a writer of horror stories or a teller of monster tales. Fishes with large eyes, enormous fanged jaws, and bellies that glowed in the dark. The truth of what lay below the surface of our own planet exceeded even the imagination of what Beebe himself had hoped to find. He had descended into a cold, dark world and returned with such bright revelations that he inspired generations of deep sea biologists to continue the exploration.

Scientists using submersibles can study delicate gelatinous animals in the open oceans for the first time (top), such as these jellies (background photo/right). William Beebe was the first scientist to observe the deep sea in his Bathysphere (inset photo/right).

The Midwater Zone Sunlight is bent and absorbed by water and so on average, the sunlight available for tiny photosynthesizing ocean plants, or phytoplankton, is limited to the uppermost 650 feet of water, which is called the photic zone. Below this depth is what many scientists consider the start the of deep sea. While most deep sea biologists study animals and communities associated with the seafloor, there is another ecological realm of animals living below the photic zone but not near the ocean bottom. Scientists who study the life in this area refer to it as the midwater zone.

The midwater zone of Monterey Bay has been the principle study area for a group of biologists at the MBARI. This group is lead by Dr. Bruce Robison, one of the world's leading midwater biological oceanographers. As one of the researchers in Dr. Robison's group, my research focused on the cephalopods in the midwater zone of Monterey Bay.

Purple-striped jelly

The Oxygen Minimum Zone In the midwater realms around the world there is often a layer called the oxygen minimum zone, which has very low concentrations of oxygen in the water. This

zone is the result of biological processes and oceanic circulation patterns. Shallow waters tend to be rich in oxygen for two reasons: the interaction between the sea surface and the air above, and the production of oxygen by tiny plants in the sunlit surface waters. The oxygen content of deep waters tends to be replenished from cold deep currents carrying high concentrations of dissolved oxygen from the North and South Poles. The intermediate waters therefore tend to be lower in oxygen content and form the oxygen minimum zone. This zone has a great influence on the distribution of animals in the open ocean as the amount of oxygen available is critical to sustaining life. Fast-moving, highly energetic fishes are not often found in the oxygen minimum zone, and if they do swim into oxygen-poor water, they cannot stay there for very long.

Fast-moving fish predators, such as this shark (top) and tuna (middle) cannot hunt for very long in the oxygen-poor waters of the oxygen minimum zone.

Vertical Migration The daily lives of most animals are dominated by trying to finding a meal while not becoming a meal for something else. In the open ocean, there are no walls or rocks to hide behind. There are no trees in which to find shelter. There are no caves in which to escape. There is only the open three-dimensional space of the sea. There are several defenses possible in such an environment. You could be very fast, like a tuna. You could be very large and strong such as a whale. You could be very tiny so as not to be seen, like many marine plankton. You could be transparent to avoid detection, like some jellies. Finally, you could escape the sunlit waters during the day by descending into the depths, and return to the surface at night to feed under the cover of darkness. This strategy is called vertical migration, and is used by a host of midwater animals including fishes, squids, crustaceans, jellies, ctenophores, worms and various gelatinous animals.

Even in the pitch-black waters of the deep open ocean, animals need well-developed eyes to see the patterns of bioluminescence produced all around them (top and bottom).

Bioluminescence Some of the questions most often asked by people curious about the deep sea relate to vision. Why do those fishes have such big eyes if there is no light where they live? What are they trying to see? How can they see with no light? While it is true that the vast majority of the ocean is at a depth where sunlight cannot penetrate, it is not true that there is no light in these regions. There is simply no sunlight. Light in the deepest parts of the oceans comes not from the sun, but from the very animals that live there.

Bioluminescence is a phenomenon whereby animals produce light. Fireflies are terrestrial bioluminescent insects that glow in the dark. Contrary to popular belief, bioluminescence is a common feature of deep-living

An anglerfish dangles its glowing lure in the darkness to entice prey towards its deadly jaws.

animals. In fact, a species that lives its entire life in an area, which that receives little or no sunlight and does not have any bioluminescent capabilities is the exception rather than the rule. Some estimate that over 90 percent of species living in the world's deep waters possess bioluminescent abilities of some kind.

The light is produced by harnessing energy released by the breaking of chemical bonds. Some animals produce light directly, or intrinsically, using special organs of glowing tissue in the body to emit light. Other animals produce light using "bacterial bioluminescence," culturing and storing bacteria that are bioluminescent. The light is displayed within the body or may be expelled. A few animals use both intrinsic and bacterial bioluminescence.

Many animals have developed special organs for channeling and focusing bioluminescent light. Photophores may be simple collections of bioluminescent tissue or complex structures with lenses and variable openings for controlling the output of light. Some animals have photophores of different types and complexities.

Animals use bioluminescence in many ways. Some species use patterns of the light or special sequences of flashes to identify one another and potentially find a mate (a formidable task for an animal living in the vast, deep, open ocean). Some species use bioluminescence to hunt by shining light to see their prey. Others hunt by mimicking the bioluminescence of other animals and thereby attracting unsuspecting prey to the lure. For example, the anglerfish dangles a glowing lure in front of its mouth which attracts small animals. When these unsuspecting animals move in closer to inspect the glow, the anglerfish gulps them down. Some animals use bioluminescence to escape predation. A flash of light may startle a predator or temporarily blind it, giving the flasher a chance to escape.

Counter-Illumination One of the most bizarre and fascinating uses of light in the middle depths of the sea is counter-illumination. At depths just below the photic zone where plants cannot live, trace amounts of sunlight penetrate and animals are vulnerable to attack from below. Some predators have learned to take advantage of this tiny bit of light coming from the surface, and have developed eyes so sensitive that they can see the faint silhouette of a solid animal above them. They swim deep, looking above to try to detect the outline of potential prey.

In response to this threat, many midwater species have concentrated their bioluminescence on their belly, facing downward. They also control the intensity of that light to blend perfectly with the light shining down around them. Their faint silhouette disappears from view to a predator below. These animals are actually using light to camouflage themselves!

Imagine watching a housefly sitting on a lampshade with a dimly lit lightbulb. It would be easy for us to see the dark silhouette of the fly with dim light coming from behind. Now imagine that this fly was instead a kind of firefly, capable of producing and controlling the light coming from its body so as to perfectly match the intensity of the light coming from the lightbulb. We would no longer be able to see the fly and it would "disappear" by glowing. This is essentially what many midwater animals do.

Cephalopods and Bioluminescence Midwater cephalopods also use bioluminescence. Many midwater squids counter-illuminate. These squids often have a light receptor in the top of their head or body, which measures the intensity and color of the trace amount of light coming from above. Some squids control not only the intensity of their bioluminescence to match the downwelling light, but also adjust the color to some degree to help the disguise.

Some squids may culture bioluminescent bacteria in specialized sacs near the ink sac. During an escape, some of the bacteria are released along with the ink. As the squid jets away, it leaves behind a glowing cloud of luminous ink. "Fire shooting," as it is known, is used by relatively few deep sea cephalopods.

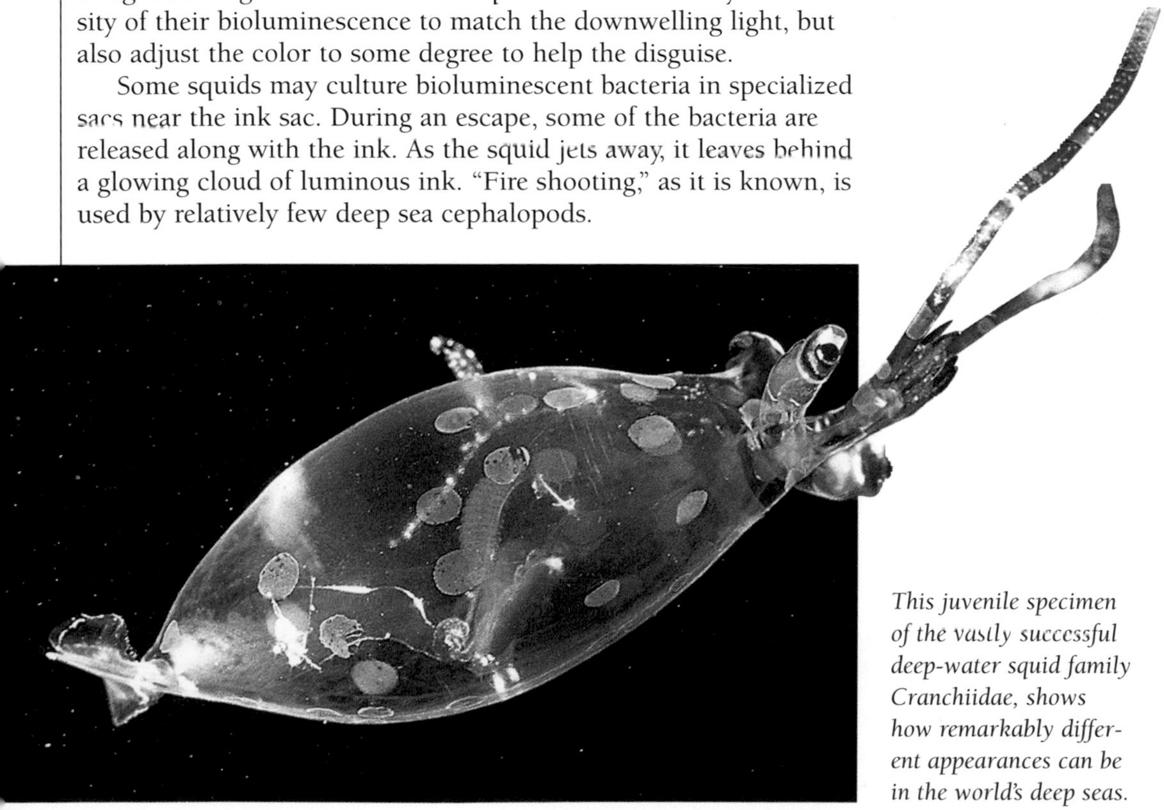

This juvenile specimen of the vastly successful deep-water squid family Cranchiidae, shows how remarkably different appearances can be in the world's deep seas.

Midwater Cephalopods

Black-eyed Squid Perhaps the most common squid in Monterey is the black-eyed squid, *(Gonatus onyx)*. The black-eyed squid is commonly found during the summer months around the bay, when small individuals about two inches or less in length school at depths of a quarter-mile beneath the surface.

During this stage of their lives, black-eyed squid have a nearly transparent body, although they produce a wide array of stripes and patterns over their body using their color organs. The arms are often red or orange, and two dark spots appear above the eyes. From below, the eyes appear black or deep brown.

Schools of over 50 black-eyed squid have been observed by using submersibles equipped with cameras. *Gonatus* is a very active swimmer and quickly flees the approach of the submersible or of other animals. After individuals reach a length of about three or four inches, they begin to descend deeper into the water, to depths of about a half mile. They also begin to live solitary lives.

During this later life stage, the body of the squid becomes translucent white although the color patterns remain. The black-eyed squid is also a strong vertical migrator ascending to 500 feet or less at night in search of food.

Gonatus onyx is a skilled hunter with a relatively meaty body compared to other deep sea squids. Each tentacle club has one sharp hook used to grasp the flesh of its prey. The black-eyed squid feeds on fishes and other squids, and probably midwater crustaceans as well.

It has no photophores for bioluminescence, relying on schooling when young and its speed when older for defense. When an individual is shallow enough to be seen and hunted by predators, the black-eyed squid will resort to using ink to escape. A small, round squid like *Gonatus* leaves an ink blob of the same general shape and size as its body, creating a false body or pseudomorph.

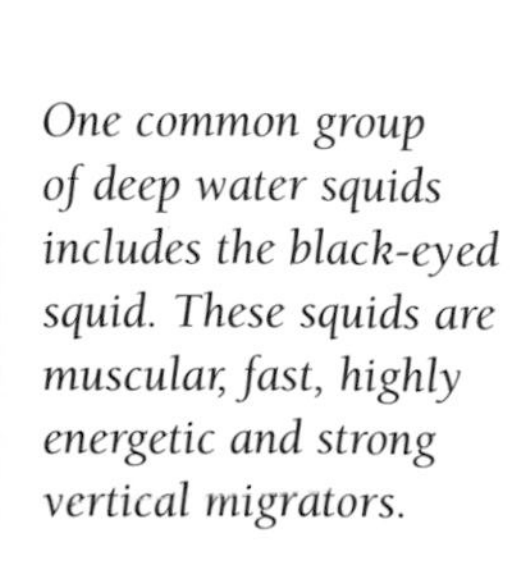

One common group of deep water squids includes the black-eyed squid. These squids are muscular, fast, highly energetic and strong vertical migrators.

In the open sea, a shark is hunting for its dinner. It spots a black-eyed squid hovering silently in the water, hoping to go unnoticed by the shark. As the shark approaches, the squid prepares its defense. It flushes dark brown and spreads its arms wide for stabilization. It expands its mantle wide, drawing in as much water as possible. It waits as the shark approaches. When it is clear that it has been seen, the squid ejects an ink blob and strongly contracts all the muscles of its mantle, forcing all the water through the siphon and sending the squid speeding through the water.

The predator is often fooled by this maneuver and investigates the ink, confused by the sudden disappearance of its prey. But this time, the shark is not fooled by the ruse. It spots the squid jetting away in the distance and quickly begins thrashing its tail to follow. The shark is a much faster swimmer than the small squid and is soon on course to catch it.

The black-eyed squid is now sucking water in and jetting it out as fast as it can, and it begins with each jet pulse to release another ink blob in the hopes of eluding the quickly approaching shark.

The shark draws near. But the black-eyed squid has one final trick up its tentacle. At the moment the shark makes a final thrust to lunge at its quarry, the black-eyed squid flips its siphon around and forces a jet pulse in the opposite direction. The squid has stopped its movement and changed course in the blink of an eye. The shark, which is moving very swiftly, cannot stop its motion so fast. By the time it turns around, all it sees is a squid-shaped ink blob where the squid was a moment ago.

Long and thin, the sword-tail squid has modified its structure to live in the dimly lit waters of the midwater zone.

Sword-tail Squid In the upper 1,000 feet of Monterey Bay resides a squid that looks like little more than a clear drinking straw. The sword-tail squid, *(Chiroteuthis calyx)*, is a bizarre-looking creature. It has all the features of any squid—eyes, siphon, mantle and ink sac, tentacles—but they are arranged into an animal that is so long and thin that at first glance the sword-tail squid looks more like a worm than a squid.

Closer inspection reveals that this animal is a squid, which has been stretched and drawn thin, with a long neck and long thin arms and tentacles. Yet the fins appear to be in the middle of the body instead of the end of the body as in most squids. Things are still not as they appear.

The sword-tail squid gets its name from an extension of tissue trailing behind the animal's mantle. The rigid extension—a thin chitinous rod running along its length—has a series of canals or vessels running through it, which perhaps help the animal control buoyancy.

The tail extension occurs only in the young and is broken off by the squid as it grows. Once the tail is gone, individuals begin to descend deeper into the water. The body continues to grow, and changes at this time.

The squid's neck is shortened and the head becomes more compact. The bottom pair of arms become very thick and develop wide flanges of skin for balance and stability. In grooves within these arms, the squid lays the shaft of its tentacles for a special type of feeding behavior.

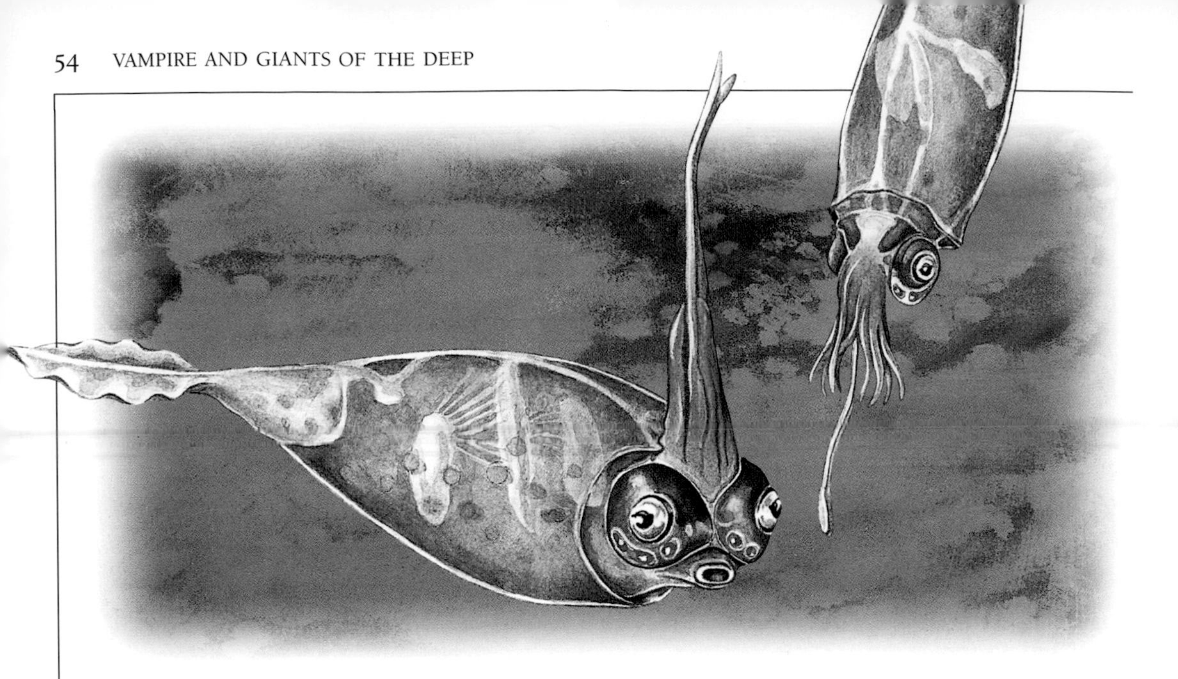

The cockatoo squid has become transparent and gelatinous, using its eye photophores to counter-illuminate the silhouette created by its opaque arms and tentacles.

Chiroteuthis hangs still in the water with its head and arms angled upward. The tentacles are slowly deployed out along the grooves and dangle in the water with the shaft lying over the tips of the bottom arms. When a shrimp or other small prey touch the tentacle club, a suite of tiny suckers holds the prey fast. The tentacles retract quickly by pulling the shaft along the grooves. The upper three sets of arms grab the food and the tentacles are deployed again for feeding. It is unclear whether or not the sword-tail squid uses any chemical or bioluminescent lure to attract small prey, but it is possible.

A series of photophores lines each tentacle of the sword-tail squid. In the dark, when the squid is disturbed, it thrusts out its tentacles and uses its arm tips to whip the tentacles to either side of its body. The entire length of both tentacles lights up with equally spaced bright blue points of bioluminescent light. It looks like a chain of blue holiday lights floating around in the darkness. The display is probably meant to deter a predator, but it is unclear exactly how the display affects potential predators.

The long, thin ink trails left behind by *Chiroteuthis* resemble the body of the squid who created them. The sword-tail squid often lays three of four ink trails as it swims slowly away from a perceived threat. This slender creature moves silently and gracefully through the water by the nearly imperceptible flaps of its fins.

Cockatoo Squid In deeper waters, below those frequented by the sword-tail squid, lives the cockatoo squid, *(Galiteuthis phyllura)*. The cockatoo squid's name refers to its resemblance to the bird during one of its typical resting positions. It hovers in the water with its arms and tentacles held together and pointed straight above its head, looking rather like the head feathers of the cockatoo bird.

The cockatoo squid is a member of the most successful (as measured by the number of species) family of deep sea squids called the

The Deep Sea

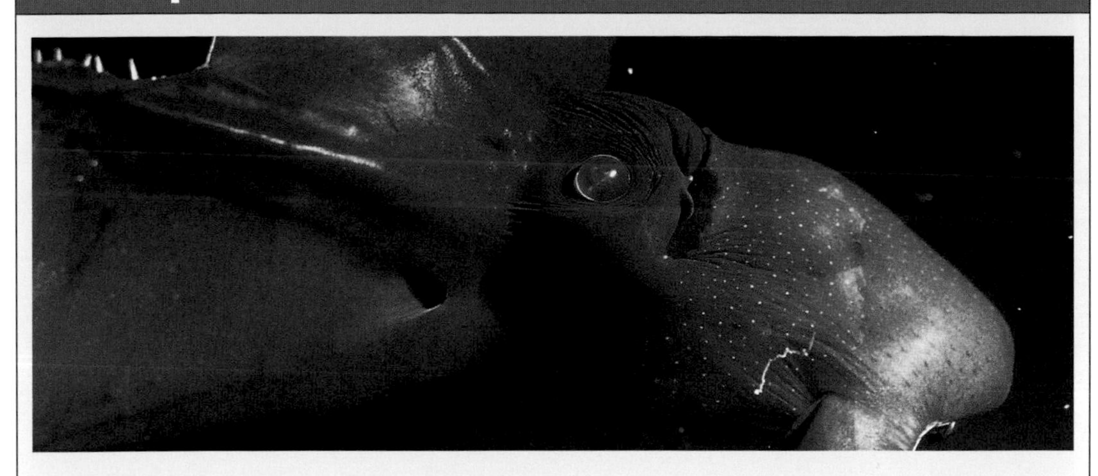

Living representatives of relict groups thought to have gone extinct occasionally appear alive and well in our deep oceans, including the vampire squid.

The deep sea is a vast open space where environmental conditions are relatively stable. Cold, dark water surrounds you. The stability of this environment has allowed some creatures to survive by avoiding the unexpected, changing conditions that exist in shallower waters. The deep sea is viewed as a refuge for ancient species, which otherwise would face extinction in the more competitive realms above.

While most deep sea species are highly specialized and have evolved to live under the unique conditions of their habitat, a few species seem to have escaped competition by retreating to the expansive abyss below. These animals are called "living fossils."

In 1938, a group of biologists working along the southern coast of Africa were amazed when they collected a living lobe-finned fish, commonly known as the coelacanth *(Latimeria chalumnae)*. Lobe-finned fishes were previously known only from the fossil record. They appeared during the Paleozoic Era about 350 million years ago. They were the dominant group of fishes during the Mesozoic Era (beginning about 230 million years ago) and were thought to have gone extinct at the end of the Mesozoic Era (about 65 million years ago), about the same time the dinosaurs were going extinct.

Bits of fossils allowed scientists to reconstruct what the coelacanth looked like, so when a live fish was found, it must have been like pulling up a living dinosaur. Although the coelacanth was found in only 240 feet of water, it served to rekindle the idea of the deep sea as a refuge for ancient species.

In 1903, the noted biologist Carl Chun collected a different sort of "living fossil." He collected the first modern vampire squid *(Vampyroteuthis infernalis)* although he did not recognize it as such. He thought it was an odd deep sea octopus and classified it accordingly. It was smooth and black with red eyes. Chun thought the black arm-web looked like a cape of sorts and imagined the tips of the filaments looked like fangs, so he gave it a name meaning "the vampire squid from hell." Quite a moniker for this shy, retiring creature.

Then in the 1940s and 1950s, Grace Pickford carefully examined the specimens of vampire squid from all over the world. Her work established clearly that this animal was unique and deserved to be put in its own group apart from the squids, cuttlefishes or octopuses. Subsequent research demonstrated the similarity between the anatomy of the vampire squid and some fossil cephalopod remains. It seemed the deep sea had revealed another living relict from the past still thriving in the darkness.

Cranchiidae. The eyes are large and the body is clear and gelatinous. The chromatophores are scattered widely about the body. It looks sort of like a brown dappled lightbulb with two big eyes. When the squid is young, its arms are very short but they grow proportionally as the animal ages. A sac inside its body along the back contains ammonium chloride. This compound, normally released as waste, is lighter than seawater and so by controlling concentrations in the sac, the cockatoo controls its buoyancy.

The cock-eyed squid is covered with rows and rows of photophores, each capable of emitting bioluminescent light (top).

The cockatoo squid ejects ink like other squids, but it also has an unusual inking behavior. When disturbed, it releases ink into the hollow mantle cavity, making itself darker. The color organs on the cockatoo squid are too sparse to color the entire body and this may be a way of replacing that ability. The entire mantle body cavity fills with ink, except for the ammonium-filled sac, which is separate from the mantle cavity. Scientists don't know if the ink of the cockatoo squid is luminous or not.

The cockatoo squid and the sword-tail squid have one common bioluminescent feature, noted first by Dr. Bruce Robison. Below the eyes in each species are large photophores. These organs are always pointed downward regardless of the position of the squid's body. In the cockatoo squid, the most conspicuous part of the body are the head, arms and tentacles. This is the part of the body seen most readily by hunters trying to see silhouettes from below. By holding the arms and tentacles straight up in the "cockatoo pose," the squid uses its eye photophores to counter-illuminate and mask any silhouette.

Cock-eyed Squid One of the most bizarre and intriguing deep sea squids is the cock-eyed squid, *(Histioteuthis heteropsis)*. This squid's most striking feature is the great difference between its two eyes. One eye is small and bluish in color and sunk into the head. The other eye is more than twice the diameter of the first, yellowish in color and sticks out from the head. There have been many ideas for why the eyes are so different, but the most widely accepted one claims that the large eye is specialized for seeing in shallow water and the small eye for seeing in deep water.

The cock-eyed squid looks like a giant strawberry. It is covered with tiny white photophores arranged in oblique rows. *Histioteuthis* uses this array of photophores to counter-illuminate. It needs the photophores to cover its muscular, deep-red body. The squid lacks the ability to change color. If it couldn't camouflage itself from below with the photophores, it would be very vulnerable to attack.

Jumbo Squids Although the true giant squid belongs to the genus *Architeuthis,* several other species reach considerable size and are sometimes called giant or jumbo squids. *Moroteuthis robusta* is one such species. The longest recorded specimen was nearly 15-feet long which, although considerably shorter than 60-foot long *Architeuthis dux,* is still a formidable and foreboding creature to behold.

Moroteuthis is a muscular squid, colored a beautiful deep orange along the top and white along the bottom. Its tentacle clubs are long and slender and lined with many hooks, suggesting that this squid is an important predator in the deep sea. It is very rare to see *Moroteuthis,* as it lives very deep and moves quickly to elude danger. Yet during the last weekend of October 1995, three specimens of

The true nature of giant squids remains a mystery. Researchers have not seen these magnificent creatures, Moroteuthis *or* Architeuthis *alive in their own habitat, but developing technologies and dedicated scientists hope to learn all we can from specimens washed ashore. An enormous* Moroteuthis *(bottom) seems to dwarf the diver swimming alongside.*

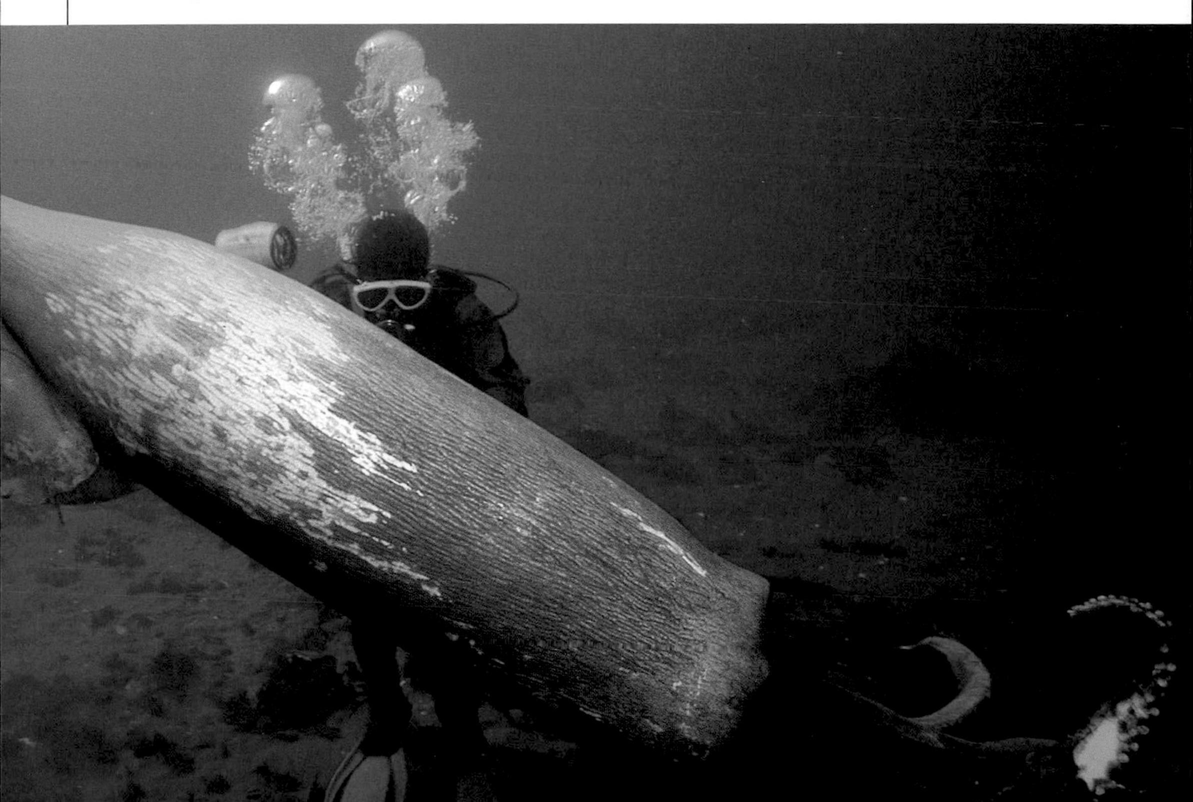

Moroteuthis were found in Monterey Bay. One was viewed and videotaped by MBARI's ROV. No one is sure why these creatures left the deeper parts of the canyon during that period.

Perhaps no animal better represents the vast amounts of information on the verge of being discovered from our deep oceans than the vampire squid. Everything about Vampyroteuthis, *including its very existence, gives us new insights into adaptations to deep sea environments.*

Vampire Squid The vampire squid is unique among the world's living cephalopods and is the sole species in its own group, having some features of squids, octopuses and cuttlefishes. It is a living fossil and by using submersibles to study its behavior, we are starting to learn more about this amazing and enigmatic animal.

Our encounters with this remarkable creature often caused a flurry of excitement. The ROV would glide through open blue water, white flecks of marine snow whizzing by. Suddenly, a tiny red ball appears on the screen. At first glance it looks like a jelly. But then we see the trace of a white whiplike filament trailing from it. Soon it begins to move in graceful and quick swirls uncharacteristic of a jelly and exposing the true identity of the animal, the vampire squid.

We pull in for a closer look. *Vampyroteuthis* hovers in the water column, peering back at our camera with its bright blue eyes. It turns itself towards the ROV with a couple of fin flaps. Then it spreads its arms wide open and stretches the webbing out like an umbrella opening. The underneath of this webbing is muted black with a velvet-like sheen. The light organs on each arm tip begin to glow and pulse. The arms are then pulled together and begin writhing over and under one another, the lights going on and off. In a darkened laboratory, these behaviors are very disorienting to watch as it becomes difficult to fix one's eyes on any particular glowing light.

Studies in Monterey Bay reveal that the vampire squid prefers the oxygen minimum zone. Perhaps the vampire squid avoids predators by being adapted to live in oxygen-poor areas. Fast-moving fishes and sharks may not be able to hunt for very long in this zone as their activity would soon require them to move to where more oxygen was available. However, some seals and sea lions or other marine mammals, which carry their oxygen from the surface may benefit by hunting at this depth.

The juveniles of the species have an extra pair of fins that are resorbed into the body as the vampire squid matures. The filaments can extend some six or seven times the total body length and help detect the presence of other animals in the water.

The vampire squid deploys its filaments one at a time. After deploying a filament, the cephalopod drifts for several minutes. If a prey animal contacts the filament, the vampire squid swims in a sweeping arc around to where the contact was made. If the squid contacts a larger animal the vampire squid quickly retracts the filament and swims away.

Vampire squids were thought to be rather sluggish, slow-moving creatures. This is true if you compare them to their active cousins, like the market squid. But *Vampyroteuthis* can accelerate and swim at speeds comparable and often faster than many deep-water squids and octopuses.

Legends of the Deep

Illustrations of the mythic cephalopods of the past (top and near right), and one true life "giant," (Moroteuthis), *(far right).*

During the Middle Ages, Norwegian fishermen sailed farther out into the open sea than most European sailors dared to venture. They returned with stories of magnificent and colossal sea monsters including the legend of the Kraken, an enormous octopus intent on dragging ships to the depths and dining on the unfortunate sailors. The body of the Kraken was said to have horns as tall as the masts of a ship and the first reports were of a writhing beast over 1-½ miles long!

Since that time, the lure and lore surrounding giant squids and octopuses has held human intrigue. Stories like Victor Hugo's *Toilers of the Sea,* and Jules Verne's *Twenty Thousand Leagues Under the Sea* increased the myth that menacing beasts lie in wait for us deep below the surface of the sea. Verne's story was made into a popular movie in which one of the most memorable highlights is a battle of might and wits between Captain Nemo and a giant squid. The story exaggerated the size and manner of the real-life giant squids, and vilified the squid in much the same way that "King Kong" vilified and exaggerated the shy and gentle gorilla. Stories of giant squid still sweep popular attention such as the novel *The Beast,* by Peter Benchley, author of *Jaws.* These stories all have several things in common: all were exciting to read, centered on species that were not mythical, and contained little truth regarding the actual biology or behavior of sharks or squids.

The truth about the giant squid is exciting enough without any exaggeration. The giant squid *(Architeuthis dux)* is an enigma. It has never been seen alive in its natural habitat and most of the information we have about it has come from specimens washed ashore, pieces caught by chance, and the remains found in the stomachs of predators such as the sperm whale.

The first estimates of the upper size limit of *Architeuthis* were inflated. This is because the estimates were made using sucker marks nearly a foot in diameter found on sperm whale carcasses. Estimates were made by measuring the sucker diameters and body lengths of the few *Architeuthis* specimens

available, and extrapolating the size of an animal, which would have been capable of leaving a twelve-inch diameter sucker scar on a sperm whale hide. Unfortunately, it was discovered later that the size of sucker scars on sperm whales was inaccurate because the scarred ring expanded as the whale grew. It was impossible to say for sure how large the sucker of the squid was when the mark was originally made.

The longest recorded specimen of *Architeuthis* is about 60-feet long. About half of that length comes from the two long tentacles stretching in front of the body. A 60-foot long animal weighing several thousand pounds is certainly large enough to inspire awe. The composition of tissue collected from *Architeuthis* suggests that it is not an aggressive and muscular animal, but probably a shy animal that hunts fishes much smaller than itself. While it is true that the giant squid and sperm whale regularly meet in battle, it is not a fair fight. The sperm whale is the predator and the squid is its prey.

Vampire squids vary in color from deep black to ruddy brown. The eyes may be red or blue. Color differences may represent two separate species, which scientists have yet to describe. Vampire squids cannot change color like most cephalopods, nor can they eject ink.

There are three types of bioluminescence in *Vampyroteuthis*, two of which were discovered in the Monterey study. The only previously known form of bioluminescence came from the pair of photophores by the base of each fin, encircled by a ring of tissue, which can be controlled to change the apparent size of the photophores. A second bioluminescent display comes from a light organ on the tip of each arm that either glow's steadily or flashes on and off. Finally, the vampire squid can eject a mucus, which contains thousands of glowing spheres of blue bioluminescent light. These glowing orbs fill the surrounding dark water with brilliant floating specks of blue swirling around one another.

To a human observer, this display changes a visual field from pitch black to one that resembles a clear autumn night sky filled with countless stars. The kind of night in Monterey that may bring thousands of schooling market squid or a few giant *Moroteuthis* up from the deep.

Cephalopods are indeed a wonderful and curious group to study and ponder. Intelligent and alien, colorful and mysterious, cephalopods will continue to intrigue us into the future. You cannot help but wonder what other mysteries await us in the vast and deep open ocean.

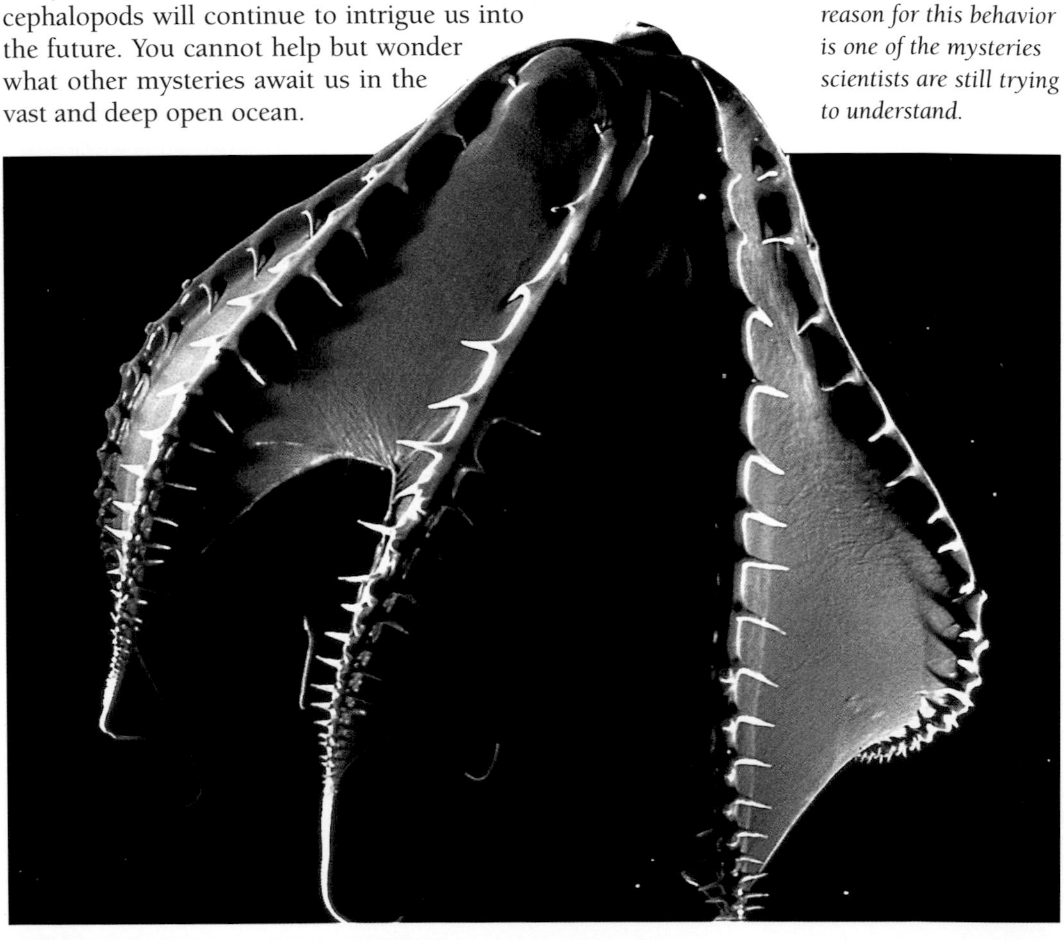

This vampire squid has inverted its body into its arms and wrapped the arms outside the body. The reason for this behavior is one of the mysteries scientists are still trying to understand.

Octopus and Squid Family Tree

I. Mollusca:
Group including snails, slugs, clams, mussels, scallops, oysters and cephalopods. Soft-bodied animals, usually with hard shells.

A. Cephalopods:
Includes octopuses, squids, cuttlefishes, the vampire squid, nautiluses and the extinct ammonites. These marine molluscs have an internal space for pumping water over the gills and out through the siphon giving jet propulsion.

1. Coleoids: an internal or reduced shell, or no shell and two gills
   a. Octopods: includes the octopuses and vampire squid, which have eight arms
      (1) Octopoda: the octopuses
         (a) incirrate octopuses: without fins or cirri
            argonaut (*Argonauta*)
            Bolitaena
            blue ringed octopus (*Hapalochlaena maculosus*)
            Japetella
            common octopus (*Octopus vulgaris*)
            dwarf octopus (*Octopus joubini*)
            giant octopus (*Octopus dofleini*)
            red octopus (*Octopus rubescens*)
         (b) cirrate octopuses: with fins and cirri
            dumbo octopus (*Grimpoteuthis*)
            flapjack devilfish (*Opisthoteuthis*)
      (2) Vampyromorpha: the vampire squid
            vampire squid (*Vampyroteuthis infernalis*)

   b. Decapods: includes the squids and cuttlefishes, which have eight arms and two tentacles
      (1) Teuthida: the squids
            black-eyed squid (*Gonatus onyx*)
            cockatoo squid (*Galiteuthis phyllura*)
            cock-eyed squid (*Histioteuthis heteropsis*)
            common market squid (*Loligo opalescens*)
            "giant" squid (*Moroteuthis robusta*)
            giant squid (*Architeuthis dux*)
            neon flying squid (*Ommastrephes bartrami*)
            sword-tail squid (*Chiroteuthis calyx*)
      (2) Sepiida: the cuttlefishes
            common cuttlefish (*Sepia officianalis*)
            giant cuttlefish (*Sepia apama*)

2. Nautiloids: species with an external shell and four gills
            chambered nautilus (*Nautilus* sp.)

Index